Dedication

To my late father, Billy Barnes. This book is for you, Dad. You wept when you said to me, "This is the hardest thing I've ever had to do," as you drove away from Fork Union Military Academy. You had the guts to risk my contempt in the face of doing what needed to be done.

I never realized it until after you were gone, so I never got to tell you that one courageous decision made me the man I am today. With this book I say: I love you and thank you for making a parental determination that has instilled in me the virtue of discipline.

Your Grateful Son,
Myers

MYERS BARNES

SUPERCHARGED SALES

BREAKTHROUGH IDEAS FOR BIG NUMBERS IN NEW HOME SALES

SUPERCHARGED SALES:
BREAKTHROUGH IDEAS FOR BIG NUMBERS IN NEW HOME SALES

MYERS BARNES

ISBN 0-9754212-5-5
© 2005 by Myers Barnes

Library of Congress Control Number: 2005920927

Disclaimer
This publication is designed to provide accurate and authoritative information in regard to the subject matter covered. It is sold with the understanding that the publisher is not engaged in rendering legal, accounting, or other professional service. If legal advice or other expert assistance is required the services of a competent professional person should be sought.

—From a Declaration of Principles jointly adopted by a Committee of the American Bar Association and Committee of Publishers and Associations.

For more information, please contact:
MBA Publishing
PO BOX 50
Kitty Hawk, NC 27949
www.myersbarnes.com

Contents

3 TECHNIQUE

4 INNOVATION

5 SERVICE

6 PERSEVERANCE

SUPERCHARGED SALES
BREAKTHROUGH IDEAS FOR BIG NUMBERS IN NEW HOME SALES

MYERS BARNES

Introduction

Taking your career to the next level requires a commitment from you.

In *Supercharged Sales*, I'm sharing with you the inspiration, motivation, and techniques to get you started on boosting your closing numbers. You'll also benefit from the innovation, service, and perserverance 'sales quicks' I've personally selected for *Supercharged Sales* to keep you speeding down the pathway of sales success.

INSPIRATION

"ALL OF OUR DREAMS CAN COME TRUE—IF WE HAVE THE COURAGE TO PURSUE THEM."

WALT DISNEY

INSPIRATION 1

Develop a Slight Edge

More than a dozen years ago I was introduced to "the slight edge" concept of business. So what is the slight edge and how do you obtain it?

In sports, business, and all walks of life, the organization or person who wins (however you define winning) isn't necessarily one hundred times, or even ten times, better than the competition. Winners generally are not even extraordinary people. The winning competitor just tends to be a little better at the important things, and does them in an extraordinary fashion. Let me give you an example:

The baseball hitter who hits over a .300 batting average will earn at least ten times as much as a player who hits .250. Yet, the difference between the two players is only one additional hit every twenty times at bat. That's all!

You don't have to be obsessively productive to be a sales superstar. Simply exceed expectations from the customer's point of reference on a consistent basis and you are the winner. Bottom line: Success doesn't always require major sacrifice. Just routinely close one additional prospect out of 20 tries. Your closing average will jump from 5 percent to 10 percent, and you'll have sales that are out of the ballpark.

SUCCESS DOESN'T ALWAYS REQUIRE MAJOR SACRIFICE.

Lessons from a Tightrope Walker

During the 1800s there was a famous tightrope walker known as Blondin (Jean François Gravelet). Blondin earned notoriety by being the first person to cross the gorge of the Niagara Falls by tightrope. He did this many times, usually without the aid of a safety net.

Blondin's most ambitious and dangerous attempt was to push a wheelbarrow loaded with a heavy sack of cement across the great falls. With the extra weight, the slightest miscalculation could topple the wheelbarrow and drop him into the falls 160 feet below. Needless to say, thousands watched in amazement as he made his way across, one foot in front of the other, oblivious to the danger of the raging waters.

When he reached the other side, the crowd cheered uncontrollably at his remarkable feat. When Blondin addressed the crowd, he challenged a nearby reporter asking, "Do you believe I can do anything on a tightrope?"

The reporter replied, "Yes, Mr. Blondin. After what I have seen, I believe you can do anything on a tightrope."

Blondin challenged, "Then instead of a sack of cement, do you believe I could put a man in the wheelbarrow, and without a net, wheel him to the other side?"

"Yes sir, Mr. Blondin. I believe," replied the reporter.

"Good," said Blondin. "Then get in!" The reporter quickly disappeared into the crowd. After all, it's one thing to believe, but another thing to actually have that kind of faith in another person.

Yet, one person did have that kind of faith, and the brave

volunteer agreed to get into the wheelbarrow and cross the falls, resting his faith with Blondin.

This time, Blondin pushed his way back across the falls with an obviously nervous passenger in the wheelbarrow. Wagers were flying, and it looked as if Blondin would successfully perform another of his conquests across the dangerous chasm. When they were halfway across the 1,600-foot rope, a man with a heavy bet who was about to lose a wager crept over and cut one of the guide wires. The tightrope pitched and Blondin fought to keep his balance, realizing he could be seconds from death. Thinking quickly, Blondin commanded his passenger to stand up and grab his shoulders.

Blondin's passenger was paralyzed. He again commanded, "Stand up. Let go of the wheelbarrow! Do it or we die." Somehow, the passenger managed to stand up. Then Blondin shouted, "Put your arms around my neck and your legs around my waist."

Amazingly, the man responded, clinging to Blondin as the wheelbarrow fell and disappeared into the falls. Using all of his experience, instincts, and every trained muscle, Blondin carried the man across the falls inch-by-inch, and deposited him on the other side.

What's the lesson? It's twofold. First, whenever you attempt something that is above average—or beyond what someone else could not imagine as possible—you may rest assured there are those who will attempt to cut your guide wires. Normally, shallow thinkers, or those who are prisoners of their own comfort zone, are there to slap you with criticism, or ridicule you with laughter. And rest assured, someone is always there to say, "I told you so." The second and true lesson is that no one goes it alone in life. Everyone needs someone, and I personally am proud to shout from the

NO ONE GOES IT ALONE IN LIFE.

rooftops that every one of my accomplishments has been blessed by the valuable help of many giving people.

So whose help do you need? The rule in obtaining cooperation is to be a go-giver, not a go-getter. The most successful people are those who have helped others obtain the things they want. As renowned author and motivational speaker Zig Ziglar says, "You can have everything in life as long as you first help others get what they want." The Bible refers to this as sowing and reaping. Socrates and Plato coined it the Law of Cause and Effect. Regardless of what you call it, if you take every opportunity to help others in life, there will always be someone to help you to the other side.

Conquering Fear

Fear can percolate through your thinking and make you the landlord of a terrible tenant. It's like a virus, permeating your body, breeding in your mind, eating away at your spirit. But fear can be the first step to something better. With a little more courage and a little more faith, you can overcome fear.

MAKE A HABIT THROUGH-OUT YOUR LIFE OF DOING THE THINGS YOU FEAR.

Ralph Waldo Emerson said that one day he was walking down the streets of Concord, Massachusetts, and a piece of paper that would forever change his life blew against his leg. It stated: "If you would choose to be happy and successful, make a habit throughout your life of doing the things you fear."

Why do people fail in selling? Fear of rejection.

So what do most people do? They avoid their fears and by not confronting their areas of concern they become even more fearful and anxious. One-third of all salespeople drop out of the profession because they cannot handle the fear and trauma of rejection. However, the top salespeople take a different approach by continually confronting their fears.

Aristotle coined the word *practice*. In its Greek form it means, "taking action consistent to the desired outcome." If you want to develop a skill—even one such as courage—you must engage in the action repeatedly until you have made it become habit. In Aristotle's own words, "If you desired a quality and you have it not, act in every respect as if you already possess the quality you desire and you will have it."

If You Think You Are Beaten

Golfer Arnold Palmer never flaunted his success. Although he won hundreds of trophies and awards, the only trophy in his office was a battered little cup that he received for his first professional win at the Canadian Open in 1955. In addition to the cup, he had a framed plaque on the wall, which, as much as anything else,

THOSE WHO WIN, ARE THOSE WHO THINK THEY CAN.

goes a long way toward understanding why he has been so successful on and off the golf course. The plaque read:

> *If you think you are beaten—you are.*
> *If you think you dare not—you don't.*
> *If you like to win, but think you can't,*
> *It's almost a cinch you won't.*
>
> *If you think you'll lose—you've lost.*
> *For out in the world you find,*
> *Success begins with a person's faith.*
> *It's all in the state of mind.*
>
> *For many a race is lost*
> *Before ever a step is run;*
> *And many a coward fails*
> *Before ever his work's begun.*
>
> *Think big and your deeds will grow,*
> *Think small and you'll fall behind.*

Believe you can and you will;
It's all in the state of mind.

If you think you're outclassed—you are.
You've got to think high to rise.
You've got to believe in yourself before
You can ever win a prize.

Life's battles don't always go
To the stronger woman or man;
But sooner or later, those who win,
Are those who think they can.

—Walter D. Wintle

He Took a Turn for the Verse

Back in the 1950s there was a well-known radio host, comedian, and songwriter in Hollywood named Russ Hamblin, who was known for his drinking, womanizing, and partying. Back then, one of his bigger hits was, "I Won't Go Hunting with You, Jake, but I'll Go Chasing Women."

One day, a young preacher came to town and held a tent revival. Hamblin invited the preacher on his radio show, presumably to poke fun at him. In order to gather more material for his show, Hamblin showed up at one of the revival meetings. Early in the service the preacher announced, "There is one man in this audience who is a big fake." There were probably others who fit the description, but Hamblin was convinced that he was the one the preacher was talking about, and he wanted none of that.

However, the words haunted him until a couple of nights later, when he showed up drunk at the preacher's hotel door around 2 a.m., demanding that the preacher pray for him. The preacher refused, saying, "This is between you and God, and I'm not going to get in the middle of it." But he did invite Hamblin in and they talked for about three hours. Before leaving, Hamblin dropped to his knees and, with tears, cried out to God.

This was the beginning of a new life for Hamblin. He quit drinking, chasing women, and everything else that he had considered to be "fun." It wasn't long before he began losing favor with the Hollywood crowd, and he was fired by the radio station when he refused to accept a beer company as a sponsor. Hard times hit. He tried writing a couple of "Christian" songs, but the only one that had much success was "This Old House," written for friend Rosemary Clooney.

As he continued to struggle, a long-time friend took him aside and said, "All your troubles started when you got religion. Was it worth it all?" Hamblin simply answered, "Yes." Then his friend asked, "You liked your booze so much, don't you ever miss it?" And his answer was, "No." His friend stated flatly, "I don't understand how you could give it up so easily." And Hamblin replied, "It's no big secret. All things are possible with God." To this his friend said, "That's a catchy phrase. You should write a song about it." And he did. The song Hamblin wrote was, "It Is No Secret:"

IT'S ALSO NO SECRET WHAT YOU CAN DO WHEN YOU'RE ON THE RIGHT PATH.

It is no secret,
What God can do.
What He's done for others,
He'll do for you.
With arms wide open,
He'll welcome you.
It is no secret,
What God can do....

By the way, the long-time friend was John Wayne and the young preacher who refused to pray for Russ Hamblin was Billy Graham.

A lesson to learn from the story: It's also no secret what you can do when you're on the right path.

Failing Forward

Every profession in the world has its own failure rate. Yet sales is the only profession where the standard, normal rate of failure can be as high as 80 to 90 percent.

In my estimation, the difference between failure and success is perception. Your perception will always be your reality. Therefore, do not perceive failure as anything other than a necessary learning experience that must occur in order to achieve success. George Bernard Shaw put it this way: "When I was young, I observed that nine out of ten things I did were failures. So I did ten times more work."

Consider the failures in the life story of this man:

Failed in business Age 22

Defeated in race for legislature Age 23

Again failed in business Age 24

Elected to legislature Age 25

Sweetheart died Age 26

Had a nervous breakdown Age 27

Defeated for Speaker Age 29

Defeated for Elector Age 31

Defeated for Congress Age 34

Elected to Congress Age 37

Defeated for Congress Age 39

Defeated for Senate Age 46

Defeated for Vice President Age 47

Defeated for Senate Age 49

Elected President of the United States Age 51

The man, of course, was Abraham Lincoln and he is a testament that success is failure turned inside out. It is critical to understand that, as you attempt greatness, you will risk failure.

FAILURE IS NOT YOUR ENEMY. That's a byproduct of achievement. However, failure is not your enemy. Complacency and fear are. For, you cannot fail if you do not try. But if you do not try, then by default you have already failed. "My great concern," said Lincoln, "is not whether you have failed, but whether you are content with your failure."

I Am Really No Different than Any of You

Billionaire investor Warren Buffet, with his usual disheveled appearance and down-home demeanor, told students at the University of Nebraska, "I'm really no different than you."

Of course, he is one the richest men in the world and runs the holding company Berkshire Hathaway Inc., which reported its highest ever annual profit on March 1, 2003.

The company showed a profit of $4.286 billion for 2002. That dollar amount and Buffet's statement is tough for a room full of college students to digest. Most of them are barely paying their bills and are dreading having to work off their college loans.

Buffet continued his speech by saying, "I may have more money than you do, but the money isn't what makes me different. If there is any difference between you and me it is simply that I get up everyday and have a chance to do what I love to do everyday. If you want to learn anything from me as a result of this speech, this is the best advice I can give you."

In reality, Warren Buffet is right—he isn't any different than the rest of us. His determination and creativity have made him who he is. As a child, he was an industrious paperboy for *The Washington Post*, covering more than one route whenever possible. To earn additional money, he collected and sold lost golf balls. At age 11, he started playing the stock market; by age 12, he was betting on horses; and by high school graduation, he owned a pinball machine business that earned him $50 a week. With his profit, he bought 40 acres of farmland in Nebraska.

After business school, he worked in his father's banking investment company for three years and as a security analyst in another firm for two years. In 1956 at age 25, he opened his own company, Buffet Partnership using $5,000 of his own funds.

Today, he explains that the main difference between him and anyone else is that, because he is rich, he has total freedom in life to do what he enjoys. But, with the exception of flying, what he enjoys is simple. He lives in the same modest house that he bought in 1958 for $31,000. He is only five minutes from his job, which he loves. He plays bridge over the Internet and watches sports on a big-screen television.

"I do spend more on my clothes. But then they look cheap when I put them on. In the end, how different is my life from anybody else's? I live in a place that's warm in the winter and cool in the summer and sleep on the same mattress anyone can buy from any furniture store," he explained in an interview.

Although he is a self-made billionaire, Buffet achieved that status by doing what the rest of us do: responding to the world around us in distinct ways according to our personality profile. The way he handles work, the way he makes decisions, the way he achieves satisfaction in work, and the way he connects with other people is not a series of random acts. His way of interpreting and living in the world around him is according to the terms of his strengths. In that respect, he really is no different than you and me.

What distinguishes Warren Buffet is how he has capitalized upon his unique strengths. First, he got in touch with his personality. Second, and most important, he used what he had to make the most of himself. He took his personality, wove in the proper education and experience and parlayed it into a billion-dollar business.

The story of Warren Buffet is relevant, not because of the fortune he has created, but because he figured out the "key to life," which can serve as a practical guide for all of us.

CHISEL OUT YOUR DISTINCT ROLE IN LIFE BASED UPON WHOM YOU REALLY ARE.

Look deep inside to identify your own particular strengths. Then, take your uniqueness, mix in your education and experience, and chisel out your distinct role in life based upon whom you really are.

Just Show Up

The lives of great men are often our best teachers.

Even if you do not follow baseball, you are probably familiar with legendary Cal Ripken, Jr. He played for the Baltimore Orioles and established himself as a legend through his dedication to the sport. Ripken broke the record for playing the most successive games on September 6, 1995, when he showed up for his 2,131st consecutive game.

What does his record have to do with new home sales? Well, to equal Ripken's record, a new home salesperson would have to work an average of five days per week for eight years and never call in sick or have any type of excuse for not showing up at model homes and sales meetings.

What's staggering about Ripken's record is that his closest contemporary competitor for consecutive starts had only played a mere 235 games in a row. Yet Ripken's ability to just show up contributed to his earning two Most Valuable Player Awards, playing 12 consecutive All-Star Games, and being named American League All-Star 19 times.

Of course, Ripken didn't just show up and sit on the bench. He hit more homeruns than any other major league short-stop, and in doing so, set himself and his family up for life. After he stopped playing baseball, he carried the love of the game into another arena. In 2001, Ripken and his brother, Bill Ripken, a 12-year major league veteran, founded the Cal Ripken, Sr. Foundation, inspired by their father's teachings and work ethic and dedication to building character through baseball. They use the Foundation as a means of reaching out to millions of underprivileged children and teaching them to use baseball as a means of developing positive character traits such as leadership, teamwork, and good sportsmanship.

Now, let's do a self-analysis. What kind of role model are you? What sort of responsibility and work ethic are you demonstrating? Does your dedication to your profession reveal itself to your employer, co-workers, and family? Or are you merely dabbling at the business? If you are doing well, I'm personally applauding you. If your are not at the top of your game, sometimes all it takes to move your career to another level is to follow the advice of actor Woody Allen: "A big part of life is just showing up!"

Show up on time. Show up to actively and enthusiastically participate in your sales meetings and company-sponsored educational training events. And show up at your models prepared with a Cal Ripken work ethic, which is as rare in business today as it was in baseball in 1995.

The bottom line is that you are judged by what you do; not by what you say you will do. Leaders like Cal

YOU ARE JUDGED BY WHAT YOU DO; NOT BY WHAT YOU SAY YOU WILL DO.

Ripken, Jr. show us how far we can go if we show up consistently and play each game to win. To quote George Bernard Shaw: "People are always blaming their circumstances for what they are. I don't believe in circumstances. The people who get on in this world are the people who get up and look for the circumstances they want, and, if they can't find them, make them."

Continue Your Personal Development

Shortly after World War II, a tall, thin 29-year-old man was hired at the Norfolk Naval Air Station in Virginia and assigned to work in one particular area of an aircraft hanger. The nation was rebuilding and, with a wife and baby at home, he knew the pressure was on to succeed.

So, he learned his job as quickly as he could and did his assigned tasks with enthusiasm and precision. He was puzzled, therefore, when one morning after he punched the time clock, he was told that he was reassigned to another location and to another job in a different hanger.

Thinking his boss was displeased with his performance, he vowed to do even better. And he did. But, once again, he reported for work one morning and found, after three months in that position, he had been reassigned again.

This happened several more times. With each change, the man thought, "I'm doing my best. But obviously the boss isn't pleased or he wouldn't keep moving me around, so I've just got to try harder."

Because he had dropped out of school in the eighth grade to help his dad support the family, he was conscious of his lack of education and concluded that his supervisor must think that he wasn't very smart.

After his sixth reassignment, the man finally approached his supervisor and asked what he was doing wrong.

"What do you mean?" the supervisor wanted to know.

"Well, I only work at each job a few months before you

move me to another one. So, I figured I must be doing something wrong and I want to know what it is so I can correct it," the man replied.

Laughing, his supervisor responded, "No, James. You aren't doing anything wrong. I keep moving you to other jobs because you quickly adapt to each one and master it. I know I can depend upon you to tackle and overcome whatever task I've assigned you to and, eventually, to come back and train others. You're a valuable employee. I wish I had one hundred of you!"

Recalling the incident recently, James, now 83, chuckled. "Here I thought I was such a failure that my boss had to keep moving me around to find something I was good at, so I kept trying harder to please him. But the truth was that each move was a promotion."

Before retiring from the Naval Air Station, James received many accommodations for original inventions he submitted, which saved the government thousands of dollars.

I share this story because it demonstrates four things:

1. Change is inevitable and often beyond your control. When it's thrust upon you, make the most of it.

2. Your perception of reality is not always reality.

3. The best way to sell yourself is through your actions.

4. Regardless of your circumstances, self-improvement is a necessity.

I'm sure you've realized, if you have ever read one of my books or attended my seminars, that the world of selling is changing every day before our eyes. New technology, new economics, new markets emerge in every area of business. You must adapt to what's new in order to maintain your selling edge and achieve long-term success.

As you adjust to changes, you will alter yourself. Continued self-development is an attitude, not an event. You must never think that taking a course, listening to a tape, or even reading this book as a one-time activity. Self-improvement in the new economy is a lifestyle.

Think of yourself as self-employed. You are selling your time, skills, experiences, and attitude to yourself. Your value to yourself is represented by your income. If you want to improve your income, you must first improve yourself. So, what are you doing to improve yourself?

If you do not invest your time and resources in yourself, you may reach a point in your career where you are no longer able to increase or even maintain your income because your value has not increased and you are no longer competitive.

Aristotle wisely noted, "Excellence is an art won by training and habituation. We are what we repeatedly do. Excellence then, is not an act, but a habit." The reason James was able to adapt to each job change so quickly was because he had formed a habit of investing in himself. He knew what he was capable of doing and, even more, what he was capable of learning. He accepted each challenge of change and used it as an opportunity to improve himself.

As Lao Tzu observed, "When I let go of what I am, I become what I might be."

What Kind of Tree Do You Want to Be?

Originating in Asia many centuries ago, bonsai is the art of dwarfing trees or plants and developing them into an aesthetically appealing shape by growing, pruning, and training them in containers. After years of care, they become a horticultural work of art.

Literally translated from Japanese, bonsai means "tray planting." Both the plant and the pot form a single harmonious unit of shape, texture, and color. Every branch and twig of a bonsai is shaped or eliminated until the chosen image is achieved. After arriving in the Western World, the art of bonsai has become an enjoyable pastime, a rewarding hobby and a way to enhance our gardens.

In the rich soil of California there is another tree, a giant sequoia that they call General Sherman. It reaches 272 feet into the air and measures 79 feet in circumference. Mathematicians have calculated that if they were to cut that tree down, there would be enough lumber to build 35, five-room homes.

At one time, both a tree that became a bonsai and the sequoia that became General Sherman were the same size as a seed. The events that happened once that seeds started to grow made the difference in the sizes they achieved. As the bonsai tree grew, it received a constant regime of root and branch pruning, periodic repotting, new-growth pinching, and branch and trunk wiring so that it would grow into a human-desired shape. A bonsai is usually between 18 and 24 inches tall. The goal is to achieve a perfectly formed miniature of the larger, natural trees. Influenced only by gravity, the seed that would become General Sherman fell into the fertile soil of California. It was nurtured by the warm rains and the natural chemicals and fertilizers that were part of the soil. No one was there to prune it or stymie its growth, so it became the world's largest tree.

I believe that each of us have a similar choice. We can stymie our careers and allow others to stunt our growth or we can establish a deep root system and grow to unimaginable heights. We can be a bonsai or a giant sequoia. The choice is ours—and so are the consequences.

"YOU GAIN STRENGTH, COURAGE, AND CONFIDENCE BY EVERY EXPERIENCE IN WHICH YOU REALLY STOP TO LOOK FEAR IN THE FACE. THE DANGER LIES IN REFUSING TO FACE THE FEAR, NOT IN DARING TO COME TO GRIPS WITH IT. YOU MUST MAKE YOURSELF DO THE THING YOU THINK YOU CANNOT DO...."

ELEANOR ROOSEVELT

MOTIVATION

"EVEN IF YOU ARE ON THE RIGHT TRACK, YOU'LL GET RUN OVER IF YOU JUST SIT THERE."

WILL ROGERS

MOTIVATION **2**
CHAPTER

Sales Success is Believing You Can

Why do salespeople fail?

Because they think they will.

Sounds like nonsense, doesn't it? However, salespeople (or anyone) can succeed to a greater degree if they just change the way they think. Motivational speaker Earl Nightingale, in his best-selling tape series, *The Strangest Secret,* clarified the secret of a successful mindset when he said, "We become what we think about most of the time."

"WE BECOME WHAT WE THINK ABOUT MOST OF THE TIME."

Do you want to boost your level of success? Do you want to develop a new mindset and a better attitude? Then incorporate these thoughts into your daily life:

- You always have—and have had—the choice.

- Whether you think you can, or cannot, you're right.

- When something goes wrong, accept responsibility and get to work to fix it.

- For one year, read only positive books and materials.

- When you encounter a challenge, or face an obstacle, look for the opportunity.

- Ignore people who tell you, "you can't."

- Replace talking on your cell phone with listening to audio cassettes or CDs when traveling in your car.

- Count your blessings everyday.

- Dedicate one hour each day to learning something new. If you take one hour every day that you currently spend watching television and instead study something new, at the end of the year you will have acquired more than fifteen twenty-four-hour days of new, life-changing information.

So, here's the question: Which will count more toward your success: fifteen days of TV, newspapers, and radio or fifteen days of nourishing a positive mindset? It's a dedicated discipline that must be employed every single day. Remember, you do have a choice.

As Thomas Jefferson noted, "Nothing can stop the man with the right mental attitude from achieving his goal and nothing on earth can help the man with the wrong mental attitude."

All Things Being Equal

All things being equal—your age, education, intelligence, experience—the salesperson who inevitably moves to the top of the profession is the one who commits to personal goals more than the other person. Setting goals goes hand in hand with success and achievement in sales as well as in personal life.

SETTING GOALS GOES HAND IN HAND WITH SUCCESS AND ACHIEVEMENT IN SALES AS WELL AS IN PERSONAL LIFE.

Goals unlock your positive mindset, they release energy, and they radiate power and focus. Goals give you vision and give you the courage to begin and persist and endure. With clearly written goals you will accomplish more in a year or two than the average person might in ten years.

Sir Isaac Newton was asked how he was able to make such significant contributions to physics and mathematics in his lifetime, and he said, "By thinking of nothing else." When you reach the point of writing your goals, making plans for their achievement, and then thinking constantly about your goals, you will move from having goals to making them part of your life.

Avoid Doomsayers

A man visited a fortuneteller who looked into her crystal ball and said, "You will be poor and unhappy until you are 45 years old."

"Then what will happen?" the man asked hopefully.

"Then, you'll get used to it," she replied.

Face it. There are lots of "fortunetellers" out there who will predict nothing but doom and gloom for you. To guarantee that their prophecies come true and that they can say, "I told you so," they may even try to sabotage your success.

These people may be your relatives, business associates, friends, or even loved ones. But, regardless of what role they have in your life, you must tune them out and keep your eye on the goal.

If you listen to them, they'll plant seeds of doubt that will erode your confidence level. You'll start thinking you're too short, too tall, too uneducated, too old, or too young. You're the wrong sex or nationality. You don't know the right people, don't have enough money, and don't mingle with the proper crowd. They'll convince you that you shouldn't get your hopes up too high; that you need luck to succeed and that you're unlucky.

IDENTIFY YOUR DOOMSAYERS.

Forget them! Don't listen. Instead, identify your doomsayers. And, if they won't change and begin to encourage and support you, then *get them out of your life or at least out of your head.* Otherwise, like the man at the beginning of the story, you, too, may envision a poor and unhappy future.

What's the Worse that Can Happen?

A manager was talking to a recently-recruited real estate agent who was experiencing "prospect phobia."

"John, I notice that when a couple comes into our model home, you busy yourself behind your desk instead of getting up and greeting them," the manager said.

"Yes, I do. I guess I'm afraid of rejection," the salesman sheepishly responded.

"Well, the next time this happens," the manager replied, "I want you to have this internal debate with yourself." The manager gave John a series of questions to recite to himself when the next prospect walked through the door.

So, remembering what the manager said, when a couple entered the model home, John silently repeated the questions in his head:

- "Where am I?"

  "Behind the desk."

- "Where do I want to be?"

  "In front of the prospects."

- "What's the worst that might happen if I walk over to them and introduce myself?"

  "They might tell me to get lost."

- "Then where would I be?"

  "Back behind my desk, which is where I am now, so what do I have to lose?"

Burn Out or Rust Out

Feeling burned out? Then consider this: To be burned out means that at one point in your life you must have been on fire.

If you are burned out now, then you must have been ignited to a temperature of almost white-hot excitement, once. You were a roaring sphere of energy, enthusiasm, and results. There was no stopping you.

What? You're thinking you were never quite that hot but you're still feeling burned out?

Then consider instead that maybe you're experiencing "rust out." The doctrine of entropy means that if you are not putting energy into something to make it better, then by default, it will become worse. If you don't use it, you lose it. This law applies to anything in the universe. If you don't exercise, you lose tone. If you don't feed your mind, your mental capacity and creativity diminish.

IF YOU DON'T USE IT, YOU LOSE IT.

To see the physical results of entropy, look around you. If not maintained, paint peels, metal rusts, wood rots, concrete crumbles, and teeth decay. The same principle applies to relationships and to your business. If unattended they, too, will gradually deteriorate and you're left wondering what happened.

So, before acknowledging burn out, do an assessment and determine if, instead, you may be suffering from a severe case of rust out. Burn out is usually physical—you've pushed yourself too hard, too long. Rust out is most often the psychological result of losing passion, energy, and motivation. Your diagnosis will determine your new direction.

All Things Come to Those Who Go After Them

Will Rogers once said, "Even if you are on the right track, you'll get run over if you just sit there."

Information, knowledge, and education are only useful when put into action. In our new economy, you can't just sit there and wait for your ship to come in. You have to be willing to jump in and swim out to it before the pier rots. As the saying goes, "It's better to wear out than to rust out."

Here's a scenario you might recognize.

There were once four people named Everybody, Somebody, Nobody, and Anybody. An important job had to be

"JUST DO IT!"

done and Everybody was sure Somebody would do it. Of course, Anybody could have done it, but Nobody did it. Therefore, Everybody blamed Somebody when Nobody did what Anybody could have done.

Be a Somebody who is willing to make things happen. Follow the advice of Nike and "Just do it!"

Procrastination

Rob Mason, a friend of mine who is an architect, made a profound yet simple observation recently. He said, "Imagine a health club where everyone who paid for memberships actually showed up to use them."

What's Rob's point? Many people want better lifestyles, but don't do anything about it. One of the main reasons many never achieve better lifestyles is that they put off taking action.

Procrastination is opportunity's assassin. It steals your time, creativity, motivation, and potential.

PROCRASTINATION IS OPPORTUNITY'S ASSASSIN.

President John F. Kennedy observed, "There are risks and costs to a program of action, but they are far less than the long-range risk and cost of comfortable inaction."

As someone once told me, procrastination is the art of keeping up with yesterday.

Keep in mind that, while you procrastinate, life speeds by.

Rules for Life from Bill Gates

Microsoft® founder Bill Gates, one of the most financially successful people in the world, shared Ten Commonsense Rules You'll Never Learn in School:

1. Life is not fair; get used to it.
2. The world will expect you to accomplish something *before* you feel good about yourself.
3. You will *not* make $40,000 a year right out of high school.
4. If you think your teacher is tough, wait until you get a boss. He or she doesn't have tenure.
5. Your grandparents had a different word for burger flipping; they called it *opportunity.*
6. If you mess up it's not your parents' fault, so don't whine about your mistakes. Learn from them.
7. Before you were born, your parents weren't as boring as they are now. They got that way from paying your bills, cleaning your clothes, and listening to you talk about how cool you are.
8. In some schools they'll give you as many times as you want to get the right answer. This doesn't bear the slightest resemblance to *anything* in real life.
9. Very few employers are interested in helping you find yourself. Do that on your own time.
10. Television is *not* real life. In real life, people actually have to leave the coffee shop and go to jobs.

Your Story of Hope

Let me tell you a story, the ultimate story of hope. You probably already know it because it has appeared in every piece of literature you've ever read. It goes something like this.

One day a person like you decides to embark on a journey. It's a supernatural journey to do something out of the ordinary, something that will make a difference in the world. Although your desire is to accomplish great things and to be a hero, you're unsure of your abilities and reluctant to leave the comfort of your home.

But finally you do and are surprised to meet, along the way, a very wise man who empowers you with secrets, magic, and words of wisdom. Feeling more confident, you travel on, searching for a castle in some faraway Camelot where you will do wondrous things and find true happiness.

Armed with a pure heart and the wise man's gifts, you assault the enemy, overcome challenges, and slay the persistent fire-breathing dragon. In the end, you uncover a priceless treasure, win the admiration of many, and live happily ever after.

The story sounds familiar, doesn't it? It's been the plot of fairytales, movies, romance stories, and even biographies. That's because literature mimics life. We all hope for something better while struggling daily to overcome conflicts within ourselves and our world. We are constantly seeking to slay those dragons of doubt, to discover a priceless treasure, and to win accolades from a critical crowd. We dream of riding off into sunset to live happily ever after.

But how many of us are willing to pay the price to make the dream the reality? Wouldn't it be simpler to fast-forward past the struggles and arrive at our just rewards? Yes, it would be easier, but not better; because it is the heat of battle that forges our spirit and fortifies our soul. It is the process of fighting dragons and overcoming obstacles that shapes each of us into who we are and makes us appreciate what we have.

BECAUSE IT IS THE HEAT OF BATTLE THAT FORGES OUR SPIRIT AND FORTIFIES OUR SOUL.

Regardless of how you define success, one thing is evident: Success is not a matter of luck, accident, coincidence, or even reward for a virtuous life. It evolves from a commitment to plan, prepare, and persevere. Success does not come to you; you go to it. And although the trail is well marked, it is certainly not well worn.

Success is the result of making a conscious decision to backpack your emotional baggage, get up, step out, and start over instead of sitting out life's game on the bench. To accomplish wondrous things and to reach Camelot, your vision must be followed by a venture. It is not enough to stare up the steps—you must also step up the stairs.

How do you do that? By realizing that you are the author of your own life story. If you don't like where you are today, do a rewrite. You can have a new life if you become a new person. That means reinventing yourself, refreshing old attitudes, discarding stale beliefs, and reprogramming your thought patterns so you not only begin, but also anticipate a journey toward higher learning, self-improvement, and personal success.

My vision is to impact the lives of others who are seeking a strategy that will shatter their own self-limiting beliefs so they can become who they want to be and have what they want in life. That's why I write books, conduct seminars, and meet with clients.

My immediate goal is to impact your life, to be that "someone" Ralph Waldo Emerson referred to when he said, "What I need is someone who will make me do what I can."

As we travel the road toward success together, I trust that it will lead you to sunsets, self-reliance, and some place where you'll live happily ever after. I pray that I will make a difference in your life. You have already made a difference in mine.

Defining Success

What is your definition of success? A thousand people will offer a thousand and one different answers. Is it fame, money, spirituality, good health, or the pursuit of personal happiness? Perhaps it is none of those. Author and motivational speaker Earl Nightingale expressed success this way: "Success is the progressive realization of a worthwhile goal."

You may be rushing to achieve, but before you begin the journey toward success, take time to define it. Since our lives are ongoing realities, true success must be part of the journey. And only you can describe what a successful life means to you.

ONLY YOU CAN DESCRIBE WHAT A SUCCESSFUL LIFE MEANS TO YOU.

To do that, start now by choosing specific goals and their completion dates. Allow yourself enough time to grow and develop before reaching them. Control your destiny instead of having it control you, and success will end up being your constant companion. Become a success on your own terms. Think deeply about what it means to you and then consistently act on your conclusions and convictions. Nothing will give you more satisfaction than being the architect of your own goals as you navigate life's journey.

Note: To know more about taking charge of your destiny, refer to your copy of Reach the Top In New Home & Neighborhood Sales, pages 231 through 254.

"A PROCRASTINATOR PUTS OFF UNTIL TOMORROW THE THINGS HE HAS ALREADY PUT OFF UNTIL TODAY."

JOHN MAXWELL

TECHNIQUE

"TODAY'S PREPARATION EQUALS TOMORROW'S PERFORMANCE."

DAVID DUVAL, PROFESSIONAL GOLFER

TECHNIQUE 3

CHAPTER

Closing the Sale:
the Forgotten Art

There are strategies to follow when closing a successful sale. Yet some sales training professionals and salespeople say that to learn specific closing techniques is to revert to an obsolete era of the sales profession. It has even been suggested that closing techniques are nothing more than customer manipulation.

This simply is not true. There are many components to closing a sale and not all of them occur at the time of the sale. For example, if you create a fabulous presentation with a good script designed only to close the sale, you are not seeking a relationship with the customer, merely a one-night stand. You are neglecting the importance of follow up. If so, you might manipulate the customer into making the decision that you want, rather than the decision that would best satisfy his or her needs. You may get them once, but will they give you referrals or call you again?

YOU MAY GET THEM ONCE, BUT WILL THEY GIVE YOU REFERRALS OR CALL YOU AGAIN?

Some sales trainers believe that success in selling is a numbers game. If you make enough calls, a percentage of sales will practically occur by themselves. And they will. But think of all those sales you didn't make that you could have if you had *closed strategically with a process.* Granted, we are closing sales differently today than in the '70s, '80s, and '90s, but there are fundamentals that always have and always will continue to work. And these fundamental skills may contribute greatly to the success of a salesperson's career.

Relationship selling, partnering, and consultative selling are valid, modern-day selling strategies. However, they are not meant to *supplant* the time-honored skill of closing but rather to *supplement* it. Some buying situations call for salespeople to operate on the premise of the one-time call and close. Others may require spending months or even years working with prospects to determine needs and build trust and credibility before closing the transaction. Regardless, it still comes down to gaining commitment and reaching the final agreement, which is closing the sale.

There are, in my estimation, these six basic critical steps to a sale:

1. Meet and greet

2. Discovery/qualification

3. Presentation/demonstration

4. Handling objections

5. Closing the sale

6. Following up and following through

If you carefully analyze the six steps, you will notice that every one requires specific closing techniques and skills. As each step is completed, the sale moves toward the end result.

When Vince Lombardi assumed the position of head coach for the Green Bay Packers, he was asked about his strategy to turn around and lead the struggling team to its eventual number one position. Mr. Lombardi replied, "I plan to lead by becoming brilliant at the basics." The basics for him were passing, running, and kicking the ball. Regardless of criticism from skeptics, Lombardi never lost his focus. He coached Green Bay to five NFL titles, won two Super Bowls, and died as NFL's all-time winning coach with a .740 percentage.

The basics for you as a professional salesperson are the six critical steps to selling. Like Lombardi, if you become brilliant at the basics—including closing—you, too, can reach the top.

> *IF YOU BECOME BRILLIANT AT THE BASICS—YOU, TOO, CAN REACH THE TOP.*

You may spend a lot of time with a prospect, but in the end, if you do not close, you do not get paid. Closing is not an event that will occur on its own. Even if you have a phenomenal relationship with a prospect and you deliver an excellent presentation, you must *be prepared* to ask for the order.

You cannot delude yourself into believing that the presentation, numerous sales calls, and a solid relationship are all that's necessary to entice a prospect to buy. There must be that one final step that *only you* can initiate and complete. In any sales transaction, there must be *closure* before there's a *check*.

What is a Professional Salesperson?

How would you define a professional? For years I have heard people use the word, especially when they refer to salespeople. By asking audiences to describe one, I have developed a consensus of the traits of the "Professional Salesperson." He or she is:

- Punctual
- Honest
- Well groomed and well dressed
- Positive with a good attitude
- Disciplined
- Persistent
- Goal oriented
- Customer focused
- Creative at problem solving
- Process oriented

In reality, there are many more attributes that could describe a professional. To me, professionalism is not about what you sell but it is about how you sell it. Or, more aptly put, being a professional isn't dictated by your profession but by how you conduct yourself in that profession.

DON'T WAIT FOR THE MARKETPLACE TO GIVE YOU FEEDBACK AND VALIDATION.

Ask yourself, "How am I doing in regards to being a professional? How do my prospects and customers think of me? What do my competitors think about me?"

Bottom line: Don't wait for the marketplace to give you feedback and validation. Incorporate those attributes that you believe you should have as a professional salesperson. Then your actions will make it so. As Malcolm Forbes put it, "Looking the part helps you get the chance to fill it."

Friendly Competition?
Yeah, Right!

How do you feel about your competition? You may say, "I have a great relationship with my competitors." But think about it. Given the choice of being in business or out of business, your competitors would probably give you directions to the unemployment office before they'd direct you to a potential sale.

Friendly competition—an oxymoron—contradicts itself just like "act naturally," "large shrimp," "alone together," "dress pants," and "pretty ugly." It would be nice if the words "friendly competition" were synonymous and if all salespeople took turns, played fair, and looked out for each other. Imagine if you went to work one day and your closest competitor said, "Hey, look I got the last sale for my builder. It's only fair that the next one is yours, so here's a lead to follow up."

For those of you who are convinced that there's plenty of room for everyone, consider this: Suppose there was space for only one neighborhood in your market and a new developer was ready to set up business in your backyard. Would you still feel there's plenty of room if your paycheck were suddenly divided by two?

A little competition can keep you on your toes while too much can knock you off your feet. As with all areas of life, there's a healthy balance. Find it. And, since you will have competition, learn to deal with it and maximize its benefits. Here are some suggestions.

A LITTLE COMPETITION CAN KEEP YOU ON YOUR TOES.

• **What's the reality about your competition?** Some competitors are truly good; some will cooperate; some are highly ethical; some will trade business with you; some will help you; but most of your competitors are the opposite of "friendly." Although they aren't hostile, they also aren't eager to share profits and prospects. They will probably be uncooperative, unmotivated, and disinterested in helping you succeed. Internally, they are probably wishing you would find another profession or at least move outside their market territory.

• **So, how should you approach your competition?** Competition should not establish battlegrounds. Don't focus on the fight. Instead, learn all you can, be prepared, and do your best. Shop them regularly; know how they sell and how customers perceive the benefits of doing business with them. Get every piece of their information, brochures, prices, etc. that you can and review it. Identify their shortcomings, and strengths and then strengthen your shortcomings. Know where they stand in the marketplace. What's their reputation?

• **How should you react when you are toe-to-toe against the competition with a customer?** Never say anything bad about them, even if they criticize you in front of the prospect. Maintain your ethics and integrity, even if it means biting your tongue until it bleeds; show them respect. Ask your potential clients why they prefer doing business with the competition. Then show them how you differ; how your benefits are superior, stress your strengths. And share a testimonial of a customer who was in a similar situation and decided to do business with you.

Don't forget to follow-up. In the event you do not conclude the sale on the first visit, remember that customers are fickle and will often sacrifice price and square footage for a trusting relationship. And in the event you do not capture the sale, ask yourself: What have I learned and what can I do to safeguard against a similar situation in the future? Do I need to make changes in my presentation? My appearance? My approach? My communication skills?

What's the Real Problem?

When you meet resistance from a potential buyer, remember that the first objection is rarely the real one. To find out the deeper meaning, keep asking these three questions:

1. Why or why not?
2. In addition to that, what else?
3. Is there any other reason you can't buy today?

THE FIRST OBJECTION IS RARELY THE REAL ONE.

Eventually, you'll get to the truth. Once that happens, you'll have the opportunity to address the buyer's real objections. And keep in mind that, as corporate coach Chick Waddell said, "You aren't closing a sale, but opening a relationship."

The Prospect Said "No!"

Fail to make the sale? The prospect said an emphatic "No!" You're sure he should have bought, so what happened?

In some cases, it may have been because you failed to establish enough trust and confidence to secure the sale. Even though the truth may hurt, sometimes you should take a step back, be objective, and ask the following revealing questions about yourself and your abilities.

> **ESTABLISH ENOUGH TRUST AND CONFIDENCE TO SECURE THE SALE.**

• **Am I dressed for success?** On October 11, 2001, *USA Today* reported that after interviewing 651 sales managers, almost across the board 94 percent of those interviewed stated, "A sloppy, unstylish dresser will cause their job to be more difficult."

• **Am I on time?** Gale Sayers is quoted, "If you're early, you're on time. If you are on time, you're late and if you're late, you are forgotten."

• **Am I organized?** Did you have all the tools, support information, and collateral material at your fingertips or were you fumbling?

• **Do I confidently answer all the prospect's questions?** My friend and colleague Bob Schultz is quoted as saying, "The absolute worst closing technique is to tell a prospect, 'I don't know.' Realize when you say 'I don't know' you literally are the one doing the *be-backing*, causing the prospect to think to himself, 'Let me know when you find out, but in the meantime, I'm going to continue shopping.'"

• **Am I demonstrating my property and homes?** Are you physically accompanying prospects on the property and emotionally involving them in the selection process of their brand new homes or homesites?

• **Am I asking the prospect to own?** It's hard to believe, but the main reason people do not own is that they are not asked to buy. Up to 50 percent of all sales calls end without salespeople attempting to close even *once*. How many closing techniques and strategies have you memorized and internalized? The answer to that question will tell you how many times you actually went for the close.

• **Do I follow-up?** The undeniable truth is most new home sales occur as a result of multiple contacts. Do you purposely and tenaciously pursue your prospects?

• **How are my third party testimonials?** Do you mention other satisfied customers to build confidence as well as create a sense of urgency?

• **Are prospects asking questions that express doubt about my company or me?** Do they ask, "How long have you been with the company?" or "What happens in the case of warranty issues?"

• **Am I communicating with prospects the way they want to maintain contact?** Fact: The Internet is now the primary tool the prospect uses to shop. Are you still trying to conduct your business only by phone and the postal service?

• **Do I come across as sincere?** This characteristic is the missing ingredient in most sales conversations. It's subtle, but if sincerity is lacking, it is picked up by the prospect immediately.

• **Do I knock the competition?** Digging for dirt causes you to lose ground. Could you be making disparaging remarks about your competition to try to make your product look better?

These questions are

DIGGING FOR DIRT CAUSES YOU TO LOSE GROUND.

designed to help you evaluate your ability to create buyer confidence from customers who decided not to do business with you. If you want them to work, be honest in your self-appraisal. Then you'll be able to identify problem areas and sharpen your selling skills. Remember, it is better to say, "This one thing I do well," than to say "These forty things I dabble in."

Real World Objections, Real World Solutions

When the customer offers an objection to your sales presentation, it is really a rejection?

There are very few actual objections that are honest rejections. Most are just stalls from buyers hiding their true feelings. Why? Maybe they don't want to hurt your feelings or they are embarrassed or afraid to tell you the truth. Many times a prefabricated story (in their minds) is so much easier and less confrontational then actually telling the truth. Therefore, they'll stall by saying something like:

THERE ARE VERY FEW ACTUAL OBJECTIONS THAT ARE HONEST REJECTIONS.

- I want to think about it.

- Do you have a brochure or business card?

- I have to talk this over with my wife, husband, children, parents, friend, brother, accountant, or lawyer.

- I'll get back to you.

- I never purchase on impulse.

So, what *is* an honest objection? Frequently, these are not stated or addressed. But, most of the time when your prospect is stalling, his or her real objection probably lies within one or more of these categories: Location, competition (prospect is comparing properties), performance or warranties, financing, third-party approval, and price and square-foot pricing.

After you determine the real objection, and not the smoke screen, how can you confront it? Practice the Boy Scout motto: Be Prepared.

The Law of Size

In sales there is a universal axiom called The Law of Size, which states, "Customers really have no more than six objections to owning the home or homesite you are selling." You may hear what seems like countless objections; however, if you categorize them, you will find they normally fall into six basic topics. Figure out what those objections are before you make a presentation. Don't wait until you are involved in the presentation and then find yourself trying to make up an answer. You must be proactive and show up prepared.

Here's how the process works:

- **Identify all possible objections** by yourself or brainstorm with team members.

- **Write the objections down.** Don't think it, ink it!

- **Script potent responses.** After identifying all objections, develop ironclad scripted responses and airtight answers.

- **Rehearse the scripted responses in role-play.** Practice, drill, and rehearse until your planned responses feel natural. This is professionalism of the highest degree.

Do this and, when the predictable objections surface, you can easily, effortlessly, and automatically move to the close.

Looking Good...

Flash back to Carly Simon and her song, "You're So Vain."

Now admit it: Didn't you think this part was about you?

A little dose of self-esteem is good. So, here are a few vain,

A LITTLE DOSE OF SELF-ESTEEM IS GOOD.

all-about-you practices to initiate that won't alienate others:

- Care for yourself.

- Save for your retirement.

- Work at being healthy.

- Exercise regularly.

- Eat with the following thought: Food is only fuel.

- Drive a clean car. It makes you feel better.

- Avoid heavy perfume and cologne. Others may be allergic.

- Wear quality clothes.

- Think energetically.

- Take vitamins.

- Keep your shoes polished. It reflects favorably on you.

Is this vanity or self-esteem? You figure it out. I think salespeople who stand erect, look sharp, and smile don't look vain ... they look like they value themselves.

Three Bad Attitudes to Abolish

Negativity is always around us. It interferes with our productivity, erodes our confidence, blocks our creativity, and brings us down. We can't avoid it, but we can learn to recognize some negative attitudes and correct them. Here's three to eliminate:

1. **Feeling guilty.** Don't inflict guilt on others and don't accept it yourself. Recognize that some people use guilt to manipulate people into doing what they want. I have a friend whose mother would feign illness to elicit sympathy and control family members. A business associate who recently purchased a home was told by a salesman (not the one he bought from), "You don't want to keep your family living in a small, cramped house, do you? Don't you think they deserve better?" Guilt causes people to develop low self-esteem, to blame themselves for things that go wrong or to accept responsibility for circumstances that they didn't create.

2. **Blaming others.** When you put the blame on other people, it shows a lack of self-confidence. Everybody makes mistakes. Accept responsibility for yours and don't point out those made by others. Instead, learn from their mistakes. Remember, the *right* to do something does not make *doing* it right. As the proverb goes, "A person may stumble and fall many times in life, but they are not a failure until they say, 'Who pushed me?'"

"A PERSON MAY STUMBLE AND FALL MANY TIMES IN LIFE, BUT THEY ARE NOT A FAILURE UNTIL THEY SAY, 'WHO PUSHED ME?'"

3. **Seeking approval.** A strong need for approval from others signifies overdependence, which can cause you to do things against your own best judgment in order to feel accepted.

Five Common Selling Errors, with Real-World Solutions

ERROR #1 Failure to Ask for the Sale. The main reason people do not buy is that they are not asked to own. Up to 50 percent of all sales calls end without salespeople attempting to close ... even once!

SOLUTION: Memorize and internalize at least five closing techniques. The professional salesperson is like a professional actor or actress who has the scripts planted firmly in their subconscious minds. Master your closing dialogue (role-play and rehearse) before appearing on stage before *your* audience.

ERROR #2 Reluctance to Demonstrate Property and Homes. If the number one mistake with onsite sales is the failure to ask for the sale, then probably the second biggest mistake is failure to transition from the sales center to the property and models.

SOLUTION: You never ask permission to show potential clients your homes and homesites. Instead, you lead boldly and confidently. Top producers all say that going from the sales center to the property and models is merely a natural event. They simply say, "Let's go," and lead clients out the door. It's that easy!

ERROR #3 The Deadly Sin: Prejudging. Prejudging is not prequalifying. Prejudging usually occurs during the initial moments of meeting a client. Many salespeople attempt to determine a customer's willingness and ability to own by his or her appearance, car, or job.

SOLUTION: Consider the advice of Henry Ward Beecher: When you want to know the worth of a man, count what is in him, not on him.

ERROR #4 Apprehension to Qualify. As logical and sensible as it seems to qualify prospects, many salespeople still fail to do so. Spending time with qualified prospects is your key to a high sales volume. In fact, sales research indicates that two-thirds of the presentations given by salespeople today are wasted on individuals who do not have the resources, desire, need to own, or authority to purchase. Is it surprising that sales can be so frustrating?

SOLUTION: Simply stated, you must guide prospects through the process of discovery and identify their wants, needs, desires, financial status and parameters, who the decision makers are, their time frame for buying, your competition, and what objections might be forthcoming. For a more detailed answer and suggestions on how to implement the Process of Discovery, refer to your copy of *Reach The Top In New Home & Neighborhood Sales*, Chapter 7, pages 71 through 92.

ERROR #5 Believing There is Nothing New to Learn. Like technology, professional selling today is evolving and changing more rapidly than in any other time in history. The seed of wisdom is the realization of how little we really know. Most people who excel in their professions are not impressed with how much knowledge they have, but how much they still have to learn.

SOLUTION: A study by the University of Southern California confirms that if you were to spend sixty minutes a day reading within your profession, then:

- In 3 years you would be an authority.

- In 5 years you would be an expert.

- In 7 years you would be in the top of your field and the best educated of your generation.

If you are saying to yourself, "I can't find an hour a day to read," then consider what you can accomplish by listening to tapes or CDs while driving. If you are an average person, you spend fifty to one hundred hours a month commuting to and from work in your car. If you were to spend that time listening to educational tapes instead of talking on your mobile phone or tuning into your favorite radio station, at the end of a year you would have significantly increased your knowledge and turned travel time into learning time.

Developing Your X-Ray Vision

"Look...up in the sky! It's a bird! It's a plane! No...it's Super Salesperson!"

You have to admit, Superman was one cool mild-mannered dude. Due to his extraordinary talents, he could perform heroic deeds by being faster than a speeding bullet, more powerful than a locomotive, and able to leap tall buildings in a single bound.

But most intriguing of all, he was able to peer through solid objects with his x-ray vision to determine when Lois Lane and Jimmy Olsen were in trouble. No distance was too far or wall too thick for Superman's x-ray vision to penetrate. He used it to evaluate and respond to every situation appropriately.

One of the most important talents that you, as a salesperson, should develop is the ability to discern each homebuyer's needs and financial ability, as well as his or her wants, needs, and desires. *You need a type of x-ray vision* to penetrate the core of your prospect's emotional agenda so you, too, will know how to evaluate the situation and respond appropriately. In other words, you need to know if your prospect will qualify for the new home *before* you begin the never ending battle for truth, justice, and the American dream.

So how do you do that?

Prior to launching your presentation, your first priority and continuing mission as a Super Salesperson is to determine if the prospect is qualified to make a purchase. Qualification is your form of x-ray vision. It enables you to ask the right questions and to see through the exterior appearance of the prospect so you won't form hasty conclusions and make errant assumptions.

To properly x-ray your prospect, there are five basic categories of discovery you must pursue before you begin your sales presentation. If you skillfully ask the following five questions, you will discern how you can best lead your potential customer from presentation to close.

1. "Where do you live now? Why are you considering moving?"

2. "Ms. Prospect, how soon do you plan on moving into your new home?"

3. "Mr. and Mrs. Prospect, what investment range are you considering with your new home?"

4. "Mr. Prospect, how many people will be enjoying your new home?"

5. "Mike, have you specifically decided on a particular floor plan? What I'm really asking is, what type and style of home are you looking for?"

Invest ten to thirty minutes in asking these questions and you won't waste hours, days, or possibly months attempting to close sales with those who cannot—or will not—purchase from you.

When Joe Shuster and Jerry Siegal introduced Superman to America in 1938, they used him to exemplify hope and strength in a combative and confusing world. The average "Joe" felt empowered just watching the man of steel overcome the problems of the world. As he leaped from one adventure to another, Superman became not only a hero, but also a teacher.

It's the same with you. Prospects need a person of integrity to mentor and empower them as they wind through the process of buying a new home or homesite. And the only way you can do that is by soliciting enough information up front to make an honest appraisal of their situation.

Superman would have never battered down a wall or wasted time trying to solve a problem without first x-raying and discovering the reality of the situation and the best solution. Neither should you.

Exposing Common Sales Myths

It seems that, over the years, a great number of well-intended sales trainers, as well as sales managers, have perpetrated a number of sales myths. The concepts may have been true at the time they originated—or at least perceived to be true—but in today's economy where change, technology, and value are driving customers, the concepts are no longer valid. I'll offer a few of the most common myths with my interpretation as to why they are myths, not truths, and what the reality truly is. You be the judge and decide for yourself what makes the most sense to you.

MYTH: Sales is a numbers game. If you see enough people, you will make enough sales.

TRUTH: Sales is not a numbers game. Professional Selling is *qualified* numbers.

If you see enough of the right people (qualified prospects and referrals), you will make lots of sales. If your only selling strategy is to see lots of people, qualified or otherwise, eventually you are going to get more rejection than you can probably handle and will either quit or fail.

Debunking the "sales is a numbers game" myth is not intended to deter you from not making lots of sales presentations. Instead, you should make it your first priority and continuing mission to spend your valuable selling time with those people who are qualified to buy.

Pressed down and shaken together, what is a qualified prospect? It's simple. Your prospect must like the community, its location, the new homes or homesites, as well as have the money, credit history, emotional desire, and authority to purchase within a reasonable time frame.

MYTH: He's a natural born salesperson.

TRUTH: Were you born to sell? You've heard it before and have probably said it yourself, "That guy's a natural born salesperson." That's truly one of the biggest fallacies in sales. *Selling is a science.* And since it's a science, it's an acquired skill, and the salesperson whom you thought was "born to sell" actually painstakingly developed the skills by learning and applying the science.

MYTH: Our prospects want the cheapest price per square foot or the best deal.

TRUTH: It is a misconception that, in the case of a new home or homesite, customers are only concerned with the cheapest price. First, you must come to the realization that a new home is one of the most significant investments of their lives (emotionally and financially) and no one makes the most significant investment of their lives with their only buying criteria being that it's cheap.

Granted, you will hear frustrating responses early on, such as, "Will you take less than the listed price?" or "We're looking for a deal," or the classic, "Your competition is cheaper." What you must realize, when your customers balk at price, is that they merely want you to justify your home or homesite's value to them.

MYTH: Everyone buys for essentially the same reason.

TRUTH: People buy a new home or homesite for their reasons, not yours. Hot-button selling is based on the 80/20 rule, which states that 80 percent of the buying decision will be based upon 20 percent of the neighborhood or home's features. In other words, if your homes have ten product features with benefits, your job is to find the one or two features that represent key benefits that uniquely appeal to the individual.

MYTH: People buy from people they like.

TRUTH: People buy from people they trust. It is the level of trust between the prospect and the salesperson that provides the cohesiveness necessary to establish a beneficial relationship. Think about this: How can you like someone if you do not *first* trust that person?

Don't shoot yourself in the foot by believing in myths. So many salespeople could be much more successful than they are. All that is needed is a willingness to change your attitude and stop beliefs that fuel destructive thinking and result in counterproductive behaviors.

How about doing a little mental housecleaning this spring? Get rid of excess emotional baggage. Polish up those selling skills. Remove mindless clutter. Sweep away lethargic cobwebs. Shake off those feelings of failure. And replace those myths with visions of success.

The Ultimate Trial Close

What's a trial close? The purpose of a trial close is to evaluate and determine where you are with your prospect during your sales conversation (presentation).

Unlike a close that concludes the home buying decision, a trial close merely seeks the prospect's opinion and tests their willingness to own before moving to the final close. Asking for opinions to check the prospect's state of mind is something you should constantly perform throughout your presentation. Here's the ultimate trial close, and it should be asked *before demonstrating your homes or property:*

> "Mr. and Mrs. Prospect, before looking at our homesites, do you have any questions about the area, the neighborhood, our company and builders, or anything we may not have covered at this point?" **Note:** Remain perfectly silent and allow them to answer. You are looking for their feedback.

If the prospect does have questions, you can answer their concerns during the remainder of your presentation. However, if the prospect does not voice additional questions or concerns, you should feel comfortable that you will not receive objections surrounding the area, neighborhood, company or builder at the tail end of your presentation.

USE TRIAL CLOSES THROUGHOUT THE PRESENTATION TO TAKE THE PROSPECT'S BUYING TEMPERATURE.

Keep in mind; the benefit of the trial close is that the

prospect can answer "yes" or "no." Because you are *merely testing the waters,* you don't end your presentation. Great sales people use trial closes throughout the presentation to take the prospect's buying temperature.

More than Just a Cheap Price

Today's smart homebuyer has more in mind than just a cheap price and they are comparing the following list of benefits between you and your competition:

• **Delivery:** A person who has a pressing timeframe to move is not in a position to negotiate.

• **Location:** By survey, the number one consideration your prospect will have while shopping is the geographic range. The three keys to real estate have been and always will be "Location, Location, Location," and as the late Dave Stone said, "People will always sacrifice price per square foot and amenities for the right location."

• **Quality:** Keep this adage in mind: "Perception is Reality." To your prospect, all homes are created equal, and quality can only be conveyed by a salesperson that creates differentials by demonstration.

• **Proof:** Are your testimonials and endorsements more convincing than your competition's?

• **Features:** Do you offer more features that are included in the price than your competition? Do you convey the benefits to support the features? Do the features you include exceed the competition's upgrades and options?

• **Guarantees:** Are your guarantees etched in stone? What are your warranties?

• **Amenities:** Amenities are the outside contributions the developer builds to enhance the desirability of a community. Your mission is to be inventive and ingeniously demonstrate the amenities prior to the selection of a home or homesite.

• **Service:** Rest assured, the subliminal fear in the prospect's mind is "getting stuck." Calm those fears by reassuring the prospect that service is a priority and you won't set sail after the sale. Follow the advice of Harry F. Banks, who said,

> *"GOOD WILL PLUS GOOD SERVICE BRINGS SALES SUCCESS THAT NO COMPETITION CAN POSSIBLY UNDERSELL."*

"Good will plus good service brings sales success that no competition can possibly undersell."

Others will always sell their homes or homesites for less. Any low-level order taker can give away his or her homes, but a super achiever not only *conveys* value, but also *creates* value by shattering the idea that the most significant investment of someone's life should be bought with a "cheap" mindset.

Six Steps to Better Decision Making

Here is a simple, proven method to apply when making decisions.

1. **Evaluate your choices.** Write down your choices so you can visually judge them.

2. **Discuss your options with someone you trust.** This helps you disassociate yourself from the situation and any accompanying emotions. It also helps you confirm the information you have and get possible feedback from an impartial participant.

3. **Consider the consequences.** Ask yourself, "What would happen if…?"

4. **Determine your level of commitment.** How far are you willing to go to make this happen? How high is it on your priority list?

5. **Create a plan.** It doesn't have to be extensive, just something that gives you a way to measure your progress and chart your plan.

6. **Get moving.** Once you've made the decision, act on it. You won't know the results until you do.

"IF YOU DESIRE A QUALITY AND YOU HAVE IT NOT, ACT IN EVERY RESPECT AS IF YOU ALREADY POSSESS THE QUALITY YOU DESIRE AND YOU WILL HAVE IT."

ARISTOTLE

INNOVATION

"WHEN I LET GO OF WHAT I AM,
I BECOME WHAT I MIGHT BE."

LAO TZU

INNOVATION 4

CHAPTER

Letting Go: Your Old Way of Selling Will Not Work Forever

Remember bell-bottom jeans and leisure suits? We still wear clothes, just a different style. How about rotary phones? We still make calls, but with mobile phones.

There was a time when a fax machine was high-tech electronic communication, but electronic communication has advanced to e-mail. Brick-and-mortar stores are being replaced by websites. And, to bring it on home, we can buy a 'Hawaiian' shirt almost anywhere in the world and get everything from financing to furniture with the click of a button.

Changes in technology force us to make adjustments in the way we do business. Technology has invited international competition, so it's more important than ever to provide excellent service and to maintain high customer satisfaction, keeping the door open to sell the same customer three or four times. In other words, your customers must be so pleased with your service that they will buy from you again and recommend you to others.

To achieve results from relationships, you must become adept at blending your old and new ways of selling—take the old tried-and-true sales techniques and update them to suit today's new homebuyer. Memorize new sales scripts. Practice other ways to meet and greet your clients. Learn how to reach a larger audience via the Internet.

BECOME ADEPT AT BLENDING YOUR OLD AND NEW WAYS OF SELLING.

Develop a process that helps you attract more prospects. Find strategies and employ techniques that convince your prospect that you, your company, and homes are the only choice.

How can you combine old and new selling techniques?

Here are two examples:

1. For years you've carried a camera in your car to take pictures of homes so you can show them to prospects. With a scanner, you can transfer them into your computer and e-mail them to prospects. Even better, upgrade to a digital camera so you can transfer photos directly into a computer for e-mail or printouts.

2. You should already be mailing cards to clients on their birthdays, purchase date anniversaries, and holidays. In addition to this, e-mail them a monthly update about a community they expressed interest in, a style of home they liked, gardening or home repair tips, or new lifestyle products. Get current information online and then personalize it for your clients. This keeps your name in front of them regularly.

One absolute I have found is that the greatest salespeople of this age have the following qualities: an upbeat, positive attitude; a commitment to deliver the best service possible; current product knowledge; proven sales techniques and strategies; and a desire to succeed that propels them toward their goals. There is one more thing: Super Achievers practice selling.

Mistakes Are Your Friend

Regardless of how much you plan, prepare, anticipate, and do your homework, one thing is certain: If you are going to take a risk, learn a new skill, develop a new habit, or test yourself in a challenging situation, you are bound to make mistakes.

It's inevitable that nobody learns to walk without falling. No writer or salesperson escapes rejection. No one playing against top competition wins every match. All risk entails the possibility that mistakes will be made.

Leaders in every industry come to a personal understanding that mistakes, setbacks, and failures are a necessary part of growth and innovation. In fact, in this rapidly changing and unpredictable world, the irony is that if you are not making a fair amount of mistakes, you are playing it too safe and not taking enough calculated risks.

THE ESSENCE OF INNOVATION IS THE PURSUIT OF FAILURE.

Renowned business consultant Tom Peters put it this way: "The essence of innovation is the pursuit of failure—to be able to attempt things and make mistakes—without getting shot."

It's critical that you understand that as you attempt your own greatness, you will risk making a boatload of mistakes. That's just a consequence of achieving anything worthwhile. However, mistakes are not your enemy. Lack of initiative, complacency, and fear are your enemy.

"The trouble in America today," said Philip Knight, president of Nike, "is not that we are making too many mistakes, but that we are making too few."

One final thought. Do not think you are too old to risk mistakes by making changes in your life. For inspiration, here are a few who never grew too old or discouraged to try:

- At age 55, Mark Twain learned to ride a bicycle.
- At age 55, Tom Wolfe published his first novel, *The Bonfire of the Vanities*, and started teaching others how to write novels.
- At age 43, Brahms finally finished his first symphony, which was begun 21 years earlier.
- At age 32, William Faulkner completed his fourth novel, *The Sound and the Fury.*
- At age 68, Tony Bennett wins two Grammy's for his "Unplugged" album. He had one other Grammy, won 33 years earlier, for his recording of "I Left My Heart in San Francisco."
- At age 72, Photographer Ansel Adams makes his first trip to Europe.

Just Ask a Fool What He Thinks

Do you want to know a guaranteed way to kill your creativity? Tell other people about how you plan to make a daring change by establishing and achieving personal goals.

It's amazing how the small thinkers of the world will succinctly explain to you how your ideas and plans will not work just at the crucial time when you need encouragement to go forward from your "comfort zone" and into the unknown.

A MAN WHO WANTS TO LEAD THE ORCHESTRA MUST FIRST TURN HIS BACK ON THE CROWD.

Here are 25 of the most common responses from friends, relatives, and office workers who are envious because you are on your way to becoming something they can only imagine. When you hear them, remember this proverb: A man who wants to lead the orchestra must first turn his back on the crowd.

1. Great Idea! Let's form a committee to go to work on it.

2. Let's think about it for a while.

3. Don't get your hopes up too high.

4. Let's discuss it some other time.

5. It will never work. / What if it doesn't work?

6. Why not leave well enough alone?

7. That's not in our job description.

8. That's not how we do things around here.

9. If it ain't broke, don't fix it.

10. We tried it a while back and it didn't work.

11. It will create more work for everyone.

12. If we do it, they may wonder why we didn't tackle it sooner.

13. The competition does it that way.

14. The competition doesn't do it that way.

15. Let the competition try it first and see if it works.

16. That's not my job.

17. The boss will never go for it.

18. Hold on. We've got to run it by legal.

19. What! Where did you come up with that idea?

20. It's too late to fix it now.

21. That's the kind of idea that could cost you your job.

22. It's not in our budget.

23. Who will we get to do it?

24. It will take a long time to get it off the ground.

25. Why do we have to push things? Let's not rock the boat.

Give It Away

Many people (myself included) who now have a prospering business found that at first their new enterprise was not marked with people beating down their doors to get their products and services.

GIVE WITHOUT REMEMBERING. RECEIVE WITHOUT FORGETTING.

Take Debbie Fields of Mrs. Fields Cookies, for instance. Unable to draw people to her counter, she broke the cookies into bite-size pieces and began giving them away. All it took was one little taste and she had customers hooked for life. By first giving away what she had, she was able to launch an empire.

In my own case, several months after writing my first book, *Closing Strong, the Super Sales Handbook*, I found myself still holding on to a huge inventory. Discouraged, but not undaunted, I decided to give them away. I gave them to managers, CEOs, entire sales organizations, people just starting business, and every audience member attending my seminars. After more than 5,000 books later, I had a depletion of inventory, but no profit. Regardless, I ordered my second printing and continued to give them away. Almost one year later, I received a call from Amway—and had a single order for 23,000 copies!

You think, "That's nice, Myers. But what does that have to do with me?" Well, let me ask you a question. Do you know why the Dead Sea is dead? It's because it has no outlets. Whatever pours into it never leaves. Haven't you met people and companies like that? People who take the last pound of flesh, or work the last nickel out of you or their customers, and give nothing in return?

The platinum rule in life is to be a "go-giver," not a "go-getter." Your true success will come when you give some of yourself away. Simply put, sowing and reaping, cause and effect, dictates that first you give and then you receive the reward.

Give your time, give encouragement, give a smile, give your money. Give it away and it will come back in avalanches of abundance.

A History Lesson about Horses' Rears

The U.S. standard railroad gauge, which is the distance between the rails, is 4 feet, 8.5 inches—an odd number. Why was that gauge used?

Because that's the way they built railroads in England and English expatriates built the railroads we have in America. Why did the English build them like that?

Because the first rail lines were built by the same people who built the pre-railroad tramways and that's the gauge they used. Why did they use that gauge then?

Because the people who built the tramways used the same jigs and tools that they used for building wagons, which used that wheel spacing. And why did wagons have that particularly odd wheel spacing?

Because if they tried to use any other spacing, the wagon wheels would break on some of the old, long distance roads in England because that's the spacing of the wheel ruts.

So, who built those old roads that had the wheel ruts? Imperial Rome built the first long distance roads in Europe and England for their legions. The roads have been used ever since.

And what about the ruts in the roads? Roman war chariots formed the initial ruts, which everyone else had to match for fear of destroying their wagon wheels. Since the chariots were made for Imperial Rome, they were all alike in wheel spacing. The United States standard railroad gauge of 4 feet, 8.5 inches is derived from the original specifications for an Imperial Roman war chariot, which was built just wide enough to accommodate the back ends of two war horses.

Now, to update the story, there are two big booster rockets attached to the sides of the main fuel tank on a space shuttle. These are solid rocket boosters (SRBs). The SRBs are made by Thiokol at their factory at Utah. The engineers who designed the SRBs would have preferred to make them a bit wider, but the SRBs have to be shipped by train from the factory to Cape Canaveral and the empty, washed ones returned by railcar to Thiokol's Utah facilities. The railroad line from the factory runs through a tunnel in the mountains so the SRBs had to fit through that tunnel. The tunnel is slightly wider than the railroad track, and the railroad track, as you know, is about as wide as two horses' behinds.

So, a major space shuttle design feature on the world's most advanced transportation system was determined over two thousand years ago by the width of a horse's rear. Although there have been opportunities along the way to gradually make changes, bureaucracies live forever and so do out-dated ideas.

THE NEXT TIME YOU NEED TO APPROACH A PROBLEM FROM A DIFFERENT ANGLE, USE THE TRY-ANGLE.

The next time you need to approach a problem from a different angle, use the try-angle. Try something new. Break the mode of responding the same way just because it's always been done that way. Apply good old horse sense instead of the other part of its anatomy.

Are You One?

Whether you watch it or not, you can't help but be intrigued by one of the more popular shows on CBS named "Survivor."

At the core of the show is the question: Deprived of basic comforts, exposed to the harsh natural elements with your fate at the mercy of strangers, who would you become?

Interesting question. It sort of describes the sales profession, doesn't it? Don't you often feel alone, uncomfortable, exposed to harsh criticism, with your fate in the hands of strangers who, often, are fighting you every step of the way?

RISE TO THE TOP WHEN IT SEEMS LIKE YOU'VE BOTTOMED OUT.

To help you compete in your own territory, here are nine ways to rise to the top when it seems like you've bottomed out.

1. **Accept that, in life, you will have problems.** And you can't solve life's problems by trying to escape them. They will not go away. You must work through them or they will remain forever a barrier to the growth and development of your spirit.

2. **Practice self-discipline.** Discipline is facing the problem, working through it, experiencing the pain and frustration, and becoming a better person for having done it.

3. **Develop a sense of optimism.** This isn't to say that you should ignore the facts and go blindly forth, rather you should develop a habit of looking for the rainbows in life. This gives you emotional fuel to make it through the storm. It also

instills in you a sense of expectation.

4. **View life in the long-term.** Make a personal commitment to never consider the possibility of defeat. You will experience failure—all those who take risks do. But that's different than defeat. Failure is temporary. Giving up in defeat makes it permanent.

5. **Have a rich imagination.** Practice out-of-the-box thinking. Don't always look for simple solutions or automatically follow in the footsteps of others. Stir your own imagination and you will develop inner confidence.

6. **Increase your energy.** Survivors see hard work as a fundamental building block of success. They press on when times are tough. And, when times are easy, they fortify themselves so they'll have the energy when times become tough. A verse in the Bible expresses it this way: "If you have run with footmen and they have tired you out, then how can you compete with horses? If you fall down in a land of peace, how will you do in the thicket of the Jordan?" (Jeremiah 12:5)

7. **Don't expect others to solve your problems.** Survivors aren't whiners or complainers. They take charge of their own destiny.

8. **Have an attitude of gratitude.** Be happy for what you have. I have a friend whose 3-year-old granddaughter awakes nearly every morning exclaiming, "I happy, Mommy!" What a way to start the day.

9. **Be driven by your own belief.** Your basic principle for being in new homes sales should center on the fact that you're doing something important that creates value and

builds legacy for others. Therefore, you should not be wracked by self-doubt. You earn your living by making people happy and helping them achieve their dreams. What could be better?

Early in his career, Thomas Edison was asked what prompted his quest for the electric light. He replied, "I was paying a sheriff $5 a day to postpone a judgement on my small factory. Then came the gas man and, because I could not pay his bill promptly, he cut off my gas. I was in the midst of certain very important experiments and to have the gas people plunge me into darkness made me so mad that I at once began to read up on gas technique and economics, and resolved I would try to see if electricity couldn't be made to replace gas and give those gas people a run for their money."

Edison had a survivor's attitude. Do you?

Change Is Necessary but Not Necessarily Easy

It's a paradox. Most of us admit that we want things to stay the same but simultaneously get better. That is, of course, impossible. Nothing stays the same, including us. We improve or decline, go forward or backward, become freer or more addicted.

Change may be so incremental that you hardly notice any difference. Then, one morning you awake and realize your body has suddenly aged, your attitude changed overnight, or your interest level peaked or declined without warning.

Life is on the move, transported forward or backward by change and your reaction to it. You can't control all life's changes, but you can prevent them from controlling you. Following is a poem that has had a dramatic impact in my life in being able to understand, cope and, more importantly, manage change. Perhaps you'll find it beneficial, too.

> *I am your constant companion.*
>
> *I am your greatest helper or your heaviest burden.*
>
> *I will push you onward or drag you down to failure.*
>
> *I am completely at your command.*
>
> *Half the things you do, you might as well turn over to me*
>
> *And I will be able to do them quickly and correctly.*
>
> *I am easily managed; you must merely be firm with me.*
>
> *Show me exactly how you want something done,*
>
> *And, after a few lessons, I will do it automatically.*
>
> *I am the servant of all great men*

And, alas, of all failures as well.

Those who are great, I have made great.

Those who are failures, I have made failures.

I am not a machine,

  though I work with all the precision of one

That has the intelligence of a man.

You may run me for profit, or run me for ruin;

It makes no difference to me.

Take me, train me, be firm with me

And I will put the world at your feet.

Be easy with me, and I will destroy you.

Who am I?

I am Habit!

—Author Unknown

Change can be good, especially when it breaks unproductive habits. Habits can be good, especially when they bring about necessary change. Use both to your benefit. It will help you keep mentally balanced. As Dr. Albert Einstein once said, "To do the same thing over and over and expect a different result is the definition of insanity."

"TO DO THE SAME THING OVER AND OVER AND EXPECT A DIFFERENT RESULT IS THE DEFINITION OF INSANITY."

Getting In Means Getting Out

Lloyd Conant, one of the founders of Nightingale—Conant, the largest producer of audio programs on success in the world, came to the conclusion that "success is goals and all else is commentary."

People with clearly written goals accomplish vastly more that those without them could ever imagine. If this evidence is conclusive, why is it then in every instance and every study only about three percent of adult Americans say they have a clearly written plan (goals) for their lives? I would suggest it's because, for most people, goals do not represent the opportunity to achieve, but rather the obligation to venture beyond one's comfort zone...and nothing could be more accurate.

"SUCCESS IS GOALS AND ALL ELSE IS COMMENTARY."

A goal is a planned conflict with your own status quo. In simplest terms, reaching a meaningful goal means doing something new and leaving the familiar terrain of your personal comfort zone. Probably one of the main reasons people do not set goals is because they must be willing to forsake old patterns and push toward new behaviors.

It has been said, "Fully 95 percent of everything you do is determined by your habits, good or bad." What is a habit? It is an automatic, trained response—a predictable ritual. Therefore, your first and greatest goal in life should be to form good habits that will automatically enhance the quality of your life, as well as broaden the scope of your achievements.

Remember, goal setting is a planned conflict with your

own status quo. It's not what you necessarily need to do that keeps you from reaching what you want, but rather what you need to stop doing. In essence, goal setting is the realization that if you want a new result, you must be willing to become a new person. And that takes work.

As the saying goes, "Getting in means getting out." You cannot take on something new without consciously deciding to discontinue something old. Effective goal setting requires the courage to stop doing the things that you know are destructive to your life and career. Like the early explorers, you, too, have new worlds to explore and conquer.

So what's stopping you?

Raising the Bar

Today, you are in a unique position to accumulate and enjoy all of the rewards that new community or new home sales will offer in the future.

To do this, however, you must begin a journey—one that will increase your sales, improve your income, and involve you in merging your dreams with reality. The journey is one of change. In order to experience an improvement of any kind, you must be willing to do something different. Specifically, you must be willing to make certain changes in your life.

Think about your own personal performance. How do you rate your current skills compared to ten years ago? How about five years ago? One year ago?

If you are not making significant efforts to continually improve (change), you're falling behind. Why? Because your competition is continually raising the bar, advancing, and redefining the playing field. Want proof?

- In 1972, Mark Spitz literally dominated the Olympic swimming competition with an unprecedented seven gold medals. In 1996, Spitz would not have been able to make the team with his once record-breaking times.

- At the 1980 Olympic Games, Eric Heiden won five gold medals in speed skating. By the 1998 Olympics, his fastest gold-medal time would have put him in 40th place.

- Professional golfers Jack Nicklaus and Arnold Palmer, both high achievers in their first 100 professional starts, respectively dominated the record books. By the time Tiger Woods completed his first 100 profes-

THERE'S ALWAYS SOMEONE WAITING IN THE WINGS TO SURPASS US.

sional starts he had walked all over both Jack's and Arnie's personal best.

These examples remind us that, in our profession as well as in sports, strategies we employed last year may be outdated or obsolete today. Plus, there's always someone waiting in the wings to surpass us. As the expression goes, "When you make your mark in the world, look out for the guys with erasers."

Don't make the mistake of believing that there is nothing new to learn, or you already know it all. Personal development, commitment to excellence, and being the best in your field is akin to running a race without a finish line. It challenges us to work to become…not to acquire.

A Final Thought on Change

I live in an area where people earn a living by fishing and crab-bing. When co-workers try to change professions or improve themselves, they want to avoid the "crab in a bucket syn-drome."

When crabs are caught, they are usually placed in a con-tainer and piled on top of each other. If one crab tries to escape by climbing toward the top, the other crabs latch on with their claws and pull it down. People do the same thing, only their claws aren't as noticeable.

If you're trying to change, to break bad habits, to improve your job performance and your life, there will be those around you who try to pull you down. For whatever reason, they don't want you to escape the confines of your current exis-tence. They want to keep you on their level. Don't let them. Even better, avoid them.

To quote Mark Twain, "Keep away from people who try to belittle your ambitions. Small people always do that, but the really great make you feel that you, too, can become great."

THE REALLY GREAT MAKE YOU FEEL THAT YOU, TOO, CAN BECOME GREAT.

"THE ESSENCE OF INNOVATION IS THE PURSUIT OF FAILURE—TO BE ABLE TO ATTEMPT THINGS AND MAKE MISTAKES—WITHOUT GETTING SHOT."

TOM PETERS

"YOU CAN HAVE EVERYTHING IN LIFE AS LONG AS YOU FIRST HELP OTHERS GET WHAT THEY WANT."

SERVICE

ZIG ZIGLAR

SERVICE 5

CHAPTER

People Buy from People They Trust

I've been teaching people for years that much has changed in the sales environment. And that is true. However, one thing does remain constant: People buy from people they trust. Your neighborhood is an extension of you. Your customers must first trust you before they will trade their money for one of your homes.

YOUR NEIGHBORHOOD IS AN EXTENSION OF YOU.

So what has changed in the sales profession in the past 30 years or so? Consider these observations:

- People want you to help them make an informed decision.

- Technology is changing the way homebuyers shop.

- Prospects have easier access to information about your homes and may even be more informed than you.

- There are three major demographics of prospects: Millions of baby-boomers, millions of retired folks, and millions of people under the age of thirty-five.

- Women are in the position of influence in most real estate purchases.

- There are increased opportunities to sell to the "new" multicultural buyer.

- People will not tolerate poor quality or service; they will just do business with your competitor.

- Your prospects have an increasing number of builders and neighborhoods where they can buy new homes.

Our profession—as well as the entire world—is changing. And you must stay current with those changes to remain ahead of your competition. But do keep one thing constant throughout your career: a high level of trust.

The trust bond between the salesperson and prospect is the foundation of today's selling environment. Trust is everything, and when trust is high enough the sale will take place.

You build high levels of trust by asking questions aimed at determining the real needs of the customer. It is only when you ask piercing questions that identify wants, needs, and desires that you are professionally selling. Asking penetrating questions helps not only you, but also your customer, understand his or her situation better.

Are You a Prince or a Frog?

One day Sarah Salesman was jogging through the park when a large green frog hopped in her path. Startled, the frog at first croaked loudly and then said, "Pick me up and kiss me and I'll turn into a handsome prince."

Sarah didn't kiss the frog but stuck him in her fanny pack and continued jogging. After a few minutes, the frog yelled, "Ok! Just give me a hug and I'll turn into a handsome prince."

Sarah ignored him and kept on jogging until she got home. Then she took the frog out of the fanny pack. Once again, the frog asked for a kiss.

"Listen," Sarah told him. "You don't understand. Handsome princes are a dime a dozen but, as a talking frog, you're worth millions!"

What's the moral of the story? The frog wanted one thing; Sarah wanted another. The frog kept trying to sell her on what he wanted instead of learning about what Sarah wanted. That's why he never became a handsome prince.

Take the time to listen to your prospects instead of trying to sell them and keep an open mind. As you learn more of what they want, adapt your sales presentation to meet their needs, wants and desires. You may never become a handsome prince, but you could become their trusted friend.

TAKE THE TIME TO LISTEN TO YOUR PROSPECTS.

Listening for the Answer

In the mid 1980s companies spent 80 to 90 percent of their sales training efforts on product knowledge, with only 10 to 20 percent of their effort on actual selling and psychological skills. In essence, the successful salesperson of the past was trained to be a walking product encyclopedia, nothing more than a talking brochure.

Telling is not selling. The professional salesperson knows this and questions skillfully while listening attentively to the prospect's needs. She asks her way into a sale. She doesn't try to talk her way into it.

ASKING CLIENTS QUESTIONS ISN'T ENOUGH.

Asking clients questions isn't enough. You must listen to their responses. Then, restate the prospects' questions and answers to be sure you understand. When you follow this procedure, you not only discover how to assist your prospects in their buying decisions but you also help them analyze their own fuzzy thinking and confront their understanding (or lack of it) of relevant issues.

Six Ways to Improve Your Listening Skills

1. **Limit your own talking.** You cannot listen and speak at the same time.

2. **Listen actively by asking questions that give feedback.** That means nodding and saying:

> "Let me be sure I understand. Are you saying that...."

> "Based on what you have told me, it seems the ideal home you are looking for is...?"

> "Ms. Prospect, that makes perfect sense. Is what you are saying...?"

3. **Maintain eye contact.** Be sure you look at the prospect as you ask and listen your way into the sale. It's frustrating to be talking with someone whose eyes constantly shift from side to side, or who looks away at something else in the room. Maintaining eye contact makes your prospects feel important and keeps them focused on the conversation.

4. **Avoid interrupting.** Sometimes a pause in the conversation doesn't mean your prospects have completed their thoughts.

5. **Concentrate.** Your prospect will know immediately if your mind is elsewhere.

6. **Listen for feelings and not just ideas.** Identify the emotional agenda the prospect is trying to convey. Take notes on key points and voice your concerns and observations.

Listening allows you to discover what your prospects need and to learn why they want a new home or homesite. Is it for profit? Relocation to a new school district? Social status? Pride of ownership? Do they want to move up in the world or scale down? What are their passions? If you actively listen, they will tell you exactly what is motivating them to buy.

THERE IS NO FASTER WAY TO BUILD TRUST BETWEEN TWO PEOPLE THAN FOR ONE TO LISTEN TO THE OTHER.

There is no faster way to build trust between two people than for one to listen to the other. It is only natural we like best the people who listen to us more attentively when we have something to say that is both personal and important to our individual set of circumstances. Keep in mind, telling is not selling.

What is in a Name?

What salutation should you use with your customers when you first meet them in your model home? Mr., Mrs., Ms., or Bill?

Because there are several possibilities, negotiating the shark-infested waters of political correctness at times can be difficult. Here are some language lifejackets that might keep you afloat.

- Listen to your prospects and customers. They will tell you how to properly address them.

"This is Dr. Simon." Call her doctor.

"This is Mrs. Simon." Call her Mrs.

"This is Marsha Simon." Call her Marsha or Ms. Simon to be safe.

- When in doubt, play it safe and address your female customers as Ms. rather than Mrs. or Miss. If she wants to be called something else, she will let you know.

- To avoid offending, address customers as Mr., Mrs., or Ms., maintaining the position of formality, unless suggested otherwise. Don't begin on a first-name basis.

- "May I call you Tom?" If the body language and signs suggest more informality, then ask permission to address the person by his or her first name. Don't assume it's acceptable.

Good luck, and remember, if prospects don't like what you call them, simply apologize and address them by what they prefer.

Seven Good Customer Service Habits to Develop

Most habits are actions you have taken for so long that they now come naturally and you no longer need to think about them—like tying your shoes, for example. When you first learned, you probably felt as if you were all thumbs. Now, you can do it with your eyes closed.

Experts have found that it takes 21 repetitions for an action to become a habit. And those bad habits are never really "broken." Instead, we simply learn to build new and better habits that replace them. But to do that, we must repeat the new habit 21 times. That's one reason it's so hard to change. We try something new, but don't do it long enough for it to become a solid practice. Then, the old habit is lying nearby in dormant brain cells ready to resurface before the new habit is entrenched.

In our profession, developing good habits is crucial to success—especially when it

DEVELOPING GOOD HABITS IS CRUCIAL TO SUCCESS.

comes to customer service. Following are some basic habits every salesperson should develop to maintain a consistently high level of customer satisfaction.

1. **Be on time.** Retired professional football player Gale Sayers is quoted as saying, "If you are early you are on time. If you are merely on time, you are late, and if you are late, you are forgotten." Being on time is a statement of respect. Conversely, making others wait until you show up creates a negative impression and is disrespectful of your customer's time and

agenda. Occasionally, you'll encounter situations and challenges that force tardiness, so the cardinal rule is to notify others as soon as you know you are going to be late. The sooner you let your customers know you are delayed, the less irritated they will become. Do not wait until the last minute, hoping that it all works out.

2. **Follow up on your promises.** If I hear one major pet peeve from customers across the board, it is this: Builders and their teams promise something and then do not follow through. For example, a customer is told that she will be given a weekly status report on the progress of her new home, and then, as if the promise were a dream, no one delivers on the commitment. Always call a customer (and your prospects) back by the time you promised, even if only to report that you do not have the answers at that time, but will be in touch again shortly. Customers are so unaccustomed to good follow-through that even that kind of contact scores you big points.

3. **Under promise and over deliver.** Sometimes, with enthusiasm to give the customer what he wants or to avoid confrontation, you may find yourself promising something that is difficult to deliver. By making that promise, you have created an expectation in the customer's mind that, regardless of difficulty, he will come to expect. If you find yourself in this type of situation, your best approach is to only promise what you can be sure of and not what you hope will happen.

For example, your customers need a 120-day delivery time of their new home; yet they want to make structural changes to their floor plan. Your production history proves delivery of the home takes 135 days minus the delay of re-engineering the plan. You are better off explaining that what appears to be a small change involves an immense amount of work and, although you would like to promise 120 days as a possibility, it is not guaranteed. By promising 145 days, you avoid disappointing your customers and you may delight them if the home is delivered earlier.

4. **Go the extra mile.** Make going out of your way for your customers a habit. By doing small extra things for them, your commitment to customer satisfaction is remembered and you create a residual of referrals. By far, the best method to develop an extraordinary relationship is frequent contact. For example, buy a camera and carry it in your car. Take photos of the home under construction or the neighborhood as it changes. E-mail, mail, or hand-deliver the photos. Absentee owners, as well as local residents, appreciate pictures of their home and community.

5. **Express empathy**. No matter how strong your commitment is, you will occasionally have an unhappy customer. At such times, expressing empathy is imperative. Empathy means understanding your customer's point of view, regardless of whether or not you agree. Employ these empathetic phrases to help your customer realize you are on his or her side:

"I understand how you feel."

"I hear what you are saying."

"I'm sorry that happened."

"I see your point of view."

Even when you aren't dealing with a dissatisfied customer, it's a good practice to match the tone of your customer. Some call it "taking a psychic photograph," but basically it's taking a moment before you even say the first word to determine what mood your listener is in. Does she look bored? Is he zoning? Do they look buoyant, happy to be where they are?

If you can match their mood with your tone of voice only briefly, it helps establish an immediate connection. "Speech syncing" adds to your charisma and creates a welcomed camaraderie. As an experiment, take one day and consciously speak at the same rate of speed and tone as everyone you meet. Then watch to see how people warm up to you—how they relate to what you're saying.

6. **Treat your customers as the most important part of your job.** With all of the functions of your job—meetings, paperwork, phone calls, and so on—perceiving your customers as an interruption is normal. Remind yourself that, although the customer may not always be right, she is the very reason your business exists and the one who indirectly signs your paycheck. By focusing on your customers as the reason you work you will make them feel important.

7. **Treat your coworkers as customers.** The quality of customer satisfaction you deliver is often only as good as the quality of relationships you have with your coworkers. Results depend upon relationships, and treating your workmates as valuable customers raises the overall quality of satisfaction they deliver to the new homebuyer.

Ice Cubes to Eskimos?

At a recent seminar, an attendee gave me a sincere compliment. She approached and stated, "Gosh, you are so good, you could sell ice cubes to Eskimos." Whenever I hear this, it causes me to reflect upon the awesome responsibility a person shoulders in the profession of New Home and Neighborhood Sales.

As a new home or new community sales professional, you are involved in what I consider to be the single most important profession in our country. You help people make one of the most significant decisions of their lives—specifically, where they will live their lives. Regardless of whether you are selling a community of primary residences, second homes, or retirement homes, you are helping people select the environment that will mold and shape their own lives and those of their families.

The challenge with selling ice to Eskimos or sand to a Sheik is, of course, that an Eskimo really doesn't need additional ice and the Sheik already has an abundance of sand. You're not selling, you're conning. You're in it for the sake of the deal; not the good of the customer.

Understand that professional selling skills are not tactics of cunning used to manipulate people into purchasing what they cannot use, don't want, can't afford, *SELLING ISN'T SOMETHING YOU DO TO OTHERS.* or don't need. Professional selling isn't something you do to others, but rather something you do for them to improve their quality of life.

113

Are You Full of PS?

According to those who keep score, our intelligence quotient (IQ) only accounts for about 25 percent of our effectiveness at work. Our technical performance accounts for about another 25 percent. However, what boosts our competence level the most are our people skills (PS): how well we deal with others, manage relationships, and understand ourselves.

WHAT BOOSTS OUR COMPETENCE LEVEL THE MOST ARE OUR PEOPLE SKILLS.

Those who are most successful in new home sales have learned how to translate their knowledge into concrete people skills that provide home buyers with what they want. For example, one skill that's necessary in sales is empathy; you must be able to tune into how others feel. But making that connection won't serve any purpose unless you can convert that into a skill such as listening to clients and seeing a situation from their viewpoint.

How can you develop your "people skills?"

• **Empathize.** Empathy is your awareness of others—what they feel, what they are concerned about, what they identify with, who they are. It supplies the foundation for a how-can-I-best-help-you mentality that empowers you to anticipate and meet their needs. This helps sales managers mold salespeople into a strong, effective team and allows salespeople to read the emotional currents of potential buyers and respond accurately. Empathy is not to be confused with sympathy. You can sympathize with someone—feel sorry for their situation but when you put yourself in their shoes and look at life from their perspective, it allows you to do more than offer pity. It allows you to offer solutions. You may remember the phrase, "Give a man a fish and you feed him for a day. Teach a man to fish and you feed him for a lifetime." Sympathy inspires you to throw the man a fish. Empathy demands that you feel his hunger pains and know that tomorrow he will be hungry again unless you teach him how to feed himself.

• **Motivate yourself.** When you harness your emotions to help guide you toward your goals, you are motivated. This powers your drive to excellence, improves your performance, and allows you to take calculated risks and set achievable goals. Salespeople who are highly motivated become committed to their profession and produce the optimism necessary to forge ahead when confronted by obstacles, disappointments, and setbacks.

• **Be self-aware.** Most of us don't spend time getting to know ourselves. Or we focus too much on what's wrong—what we don't like about ourselves—and neglect to feed our soul with affirmations. Self-awareness is the art of knowing how you truly feel and being able to accurately assess your abilities. It fuels your self-confidence and allows you to feel secure in your strengths. You must have a strong sense of self-awareness to make good decisions because that is how you tap into your acquired wisdom and are able to confidently follow your gut-feeling or intuition.

• **Practice self-control.** This is your ability to manage your emotions, to stay calm, and to think clearly under stress. It allows you to be flexible, to "go with the flow," to be accommodating amid unexpected or shifting circumstances. When you practice self-control, you are able to delay gratification, act responsibly, regulate your behavior, and maintain your integrity when those around you are losing theirs. As a result, clients will trust you and you'll be more at peace with yourself.

• **Develop good social skills.** These are the verbal and nonverbal behaviors that allow people to communicate by giving, receiving, and interpreting messages. Social skills are learned behaviors influenced by a person's upbringing, age, sex, social status, culture, education, social group, and environment. Because enjoyable communication between people is one of the most important components of life, failure to learn adequate social skills may lead to feelings of rejection, poor self-esteem, loneliness, isolation, depression, anxiety, and aggression. Learning how to handle relationships adeptly and interact with others is critical to success. You can have brilliant selling ideas or know creative ways to finance property, but if you lack the social skills necessary to make the ideas palatable, no one will listen to you. Social skills are used to inspire, guide, influence, and persuade. They enhance and maintain relationships. And, most of all, they make life and sales a lot easier.

ENJOYABLE COMMUNICATION BETWEEN PEOPLE IS ONE OF THE MOST IMPORTANT COMPONENTS OF LIFE.

• **Know your strengths and weaknesses.** List them. Seek input from others. Then decide what areas need improvement. Should you be a better listener? How are your powers of persuasion? Do you have a bad temper? Are you thoughtless?

Do you tend to be rude, selfish, or easily upset? Once you identify the areas you need to improve, ask yourself: How important is this to my profession or lifestyle? Am I willing to invest enough time and energy to change this? If not, why not? Be honest with yourself and you'll be able to focus on the most important areas first.

Define the specific areas where you want to improve. To zero in, think of specific situations rather than skills. For example, if you want to be more empathic when your buyers are sitting down to consider signing a contract, think: "When this happens, I only listen partially to what they are saying because my mind is ahead of them, wondering what I can say next to make them buy. I need to be more attentive and really listen to what they are saying."

• **Be aware of your behavior when the heat is on.** How do you react when a contract goes down? What is in your mind when a potential buyer says no? Do you act irritated, impatient, condescending? Does your mind wander easily? Are you so busy pre-judging the potential buyer that you miss clues that would help you close the sale?

• **Seek out good role models.** If you have trouble listening, find someone who is a wonderful listener and watch closely. Read books about the topic or listen to motivational tapes and visualize how experts would handle this. Ask for suggestions and objective feedback from those you trust.

• **Cut yourself some slack.** If you make a mistake or lapse into old behavior, don't beat yourself up, belittle yourself, or repeat despairing messages to yourself. Consider the cause of the lapse and make it a point to be more careful next time.

How Your Customers Want to Buy Their New Homes

Curious about what customers expect from a salesperson? Based upon a survey, this is what they said. How do you rate?

- "Listen to me." Understand that listening is the first commandment of sales because listening is learning. Listening *LISTENING IS LEARNING* establishes the prospects' needs and helps you ferret out their reasons for wanting a new home. Are they looking for security? Status? Are they moving up in the world or scaling down? What is their passion? From their viewpoint, what is motivating them?

- "Give me a good reason why your neighborhood and home is perfect for me." If you have questioned skillfully and listened carefully, you will have an understanding of how to present the benefits (hot buttons) that match each customer's unique set of circumstances.

- "Show me I am not a pioneer. Tell me how someone similar to me succeeded by owning a home in this or a similar community." Few buyers want to feel as though they are the first or the only, so restore your customers' confidence by confirming their decisions to purchase. Use third party testimonials, show them a published article, and demonstrate that people just like them are happy with their decisions.

- "Tell me how you will serve me after you help me become an owner." Some people inherently don't trust salespeople because previously they have been sold nothing but empty promises. Express to them the commitment to customer satisfaction that is shared by you and your company.

- "Make sure you convey to me that the price is fair." Buyers want reassurance that the price they are paying is the absolute best value, as they perceive it. Remember, it is a misconception that customers are only concerned with the lowest price. Equally if not more important is your timely delivery, consistent follow up, faithful follow through, and commitment to your customer's best interest.

- "Don't argue with me. Even if I am wrong, I don't want to be told so."

- Keep in mind the adage: A man convinced against his will is of the same opinion still.

- "Show me the best way to pay." Of the six top fears for acquiring real estate, two of them center on financial concerns. Your customers need information and help in understanding financial alternatives.

- "Give me a choice. Let me decide, but make consultative recommendations. Don't confuse me. The more complicated it is, the less likely I am to buy. I may be nervous and need you to affirm my decision with facts that help me feel confident."

- "Deliver to me what you sold me. I've just given you my hard-earned money (security) and, in essence, have traded my money for your promises. If I give you my money and you disappoint me, I may never do business with you again or give you referrals."

- "Follow up with me in the manner in which I prefer to

communicate." Customers are beginning to shop differently. They are using the Internet to begin and end their buying processes. If that's how they communicate, don't waste their time contacting them with antiquated methods of follow up.

BOTTOM LINE: Customers don't take the time to consciously critique your sales process. They just say no. And that's a word you want to avoid.

CUSTOMERS DON'T TAKE THE TIME TO CONSCIOUSLY CRITIQUE YOUR SALES PROCESS.

Driving for a Better Price

Since the dawn of professional new home sales, the consumer has been effectively convincing salespeople that price is their most important concern. This is not a new behavior. However, the zeal with which homebuyers display their price-only mentality takes a great toll on company profits and the industry as a whole.

If you analyze this a little further, you realize that there is low cost and there is low price. There is high value and there is low value. And there is fair price and good value.

When I ask a roomful of salespeople what the number one thing is that a consumer wants today, what do you think their answer is? You got it—lower price. The majority of them say a homebuyer is looking for a lower price first, quality second and service third.

Now let's switch audiences for a moment and ask a roomful of homebuyers the same question. How do you think they respond?

The most frequent answers I hear are service first, quality second and a cheaper price third. It seems there is a perceptional difference in what a new homebuyer wants

THERE IS A PERCEPTIONAL DIFFERENCE IN WHAT A NEW HOMEBUYER WANTS AND WHAT THEY ACTUALLY TELL SALESPEOPLE THEY WANT.

and what they actually tell salespeople they want. How do you explain that? By understanding the difference between cost and price.

• **Price** is defined as what we pay for a new home. We write a check, use some of our savings, and have just bought a brand new home at a set dollar amount (price).

• **Cost** is what we will pay for the new home we have bought over a period of time.

Those who buy a cheap home will most likely have more service bills and higher emotional inconvenience—expenses that will last as long as the home is owned. They may have bought a home at a lower initial price but at a higher cost.

Think about it. When the new homebuyer says he's shopping for the lowest price, in his mind he is thinking, "I want to pay a cheap price for a top-quality home that won't give me problems and fulfill all my wants, needs, and desires." Hey! Get real! There's no such animal. In his heart of hearts, the homebuyer knows this. So, although he is mouthing this, he must really mean something else.

If you interpret what homebuyers are actually saying, it is this: They want to pay a fair price for a new home that won't give them grief in years to come. Their top priority is good service, which means they know they can trust the salesperson to "tell it like it is," to give them the information they need to make an intelligent decision and not pigeonhole them as "cheap."

In other words, when they say low price, they really want lowest cost. Therefore, your job as a professional salesperson is to question them more thoroughly on what they really want (price, cost, or value) and define the difference for them in terms of your new homes, neighborhood, and service. This is defining value. And value is always "perceived."

Each one of your prospects interprets value in his or her own personal terms. Therefore, your mission in new home sales is not to work at lowering the price of your homes, but to work at understanding how each prospect perceives value.

To effectively respond to the price-only mentality of consumers successfully, new homes salespeople must:

- Become a construction authority, internalizing and memorizing every construction definition and term.

- Know everything there is to know about the uniqueness of their homes in the marketplace.

- Know the complete needs, concerns, and wants of their customers.

- Have the skills to match their homes to the needs, wants, and concerns of each customer.

- Have a general understanding of business.

- Have high self-esteem.

- Possess the ability to manage the emotional issues of selling and rejection.

- Believe in the company and homes they represent.

Pretty tall order, wouldn't you agree? Absolutely, but the rewards can be just as big if you understand the only true secret to professional selling is this: Ask constant, preplanned (scripted) professional and probing questions and then position your homes and service appropriately in the mind of the prospect.

In new home sales, you can't stop a price-only mentality from landing in the minds of your buyers but you can keep it from staying there by helping them realize that they don't really want cheap, they want value. They don't want to sacrifice warranties, quality workmanship, square footage and livability, a lovely and safe neighborhood, interior color and product choices, amenities, convenience, prestige, and a number of other "hidden" advantages just to get a low initial price because it will cost them more in the long-run.

YOU CAN'T STOP A PRICE-ONLY MENTALITY FROM LANDING IN THE MINDS OF YOUR BUYERS BUT YOU CAN KEEP IT FROM STAYING THERE.

What they do want is a new lifestyle that doesn't include the aggravation, expense, and emotional turmoil that usually accompanies a cheaply priced home. Simply stated, they want a better life in a new home and you can give it to them. Show them that your new homes coupled with exceptional service can offer them what they really want and price will not be a hindrance.

How to Make Your Prospect Confident Enough to Buy

Your prospects will not own if they lack confidence in you, your neighborhood, or your homes. You must use sales tools, stories, and examples in a way that allows your prospects to relate ownership of your product to their unique set of circumstances.

Besides the basics—be on time, *INSTILL CONFIDENCE.* be enthusiastic, and look professional—here are methods you can employ to instill confidence:

• **Be completely prepared.** A fumbling, excuse-making salesperson builds zero confidence.

• **Have something in writing.** An article about your company or product from a national news source elevates your credibility.

• **Emphasize customer satisfaction and service after the sale.** Today's buyer wants to be certain you will not sell and skedaddle.

• **Sell to serve—not for commission.** New home and neighborhood selling is not something you do to a person, but something you do for them. Prospects can sense a greedy salesperson.

• **Ask the right questions.** Avoid bombarding the prospect with information overload. Zig Ziglar advises, "People don't care how much you know. They first want to know how much you care." The most important link to the sales process is to ask the right questions.

• **Organize customer testimonials.** Obtain letters that cover various aspects of your business—quality, service, on-time delivery. Be sure your letters answer the buyer's objections. Also, on high quality letterhead, print a list of satisfied customers.

• **Tell third-party stories of how you helped another customer in a similar situation.** Your prospects do not want to feel as if they are pioneers. They want assurance that others "just like them" acquired a home or homesite for the same reasons.

YOU EARN REFERRALS BY EXCELLING IN SERVICE.

• **Build a meaningful referral business.** Results depend on relationships. Remember that you earn referrals by excelling in service.

Make Good on Your Promises

Most community salespeople believe we sell homes and home-sites. This is only partly true. What we actually sell is a promise...and wrapped around that promise is our sense of integrity. Basically, what we say to our prospects during our sales presentation is: "You give me a check and I'll give you a promise to complete the transaction to your satisfaction. And with the promise comes my word that you will be receiving a new home of high quality, delivered on time, hassle free with no punch, completely warranted, and backed by my company."

Since we're selling promises, we must be confident that what we promise can be delivered. Sometimes in the exuberance of the sales presentation (and during conversation), we make promises with the best of intention; but something happens and we end up breaking them. We may judge ourselves by our intentions, but our prospects and customers judge us by our actions. The proverb "Actions speak louder than words" is right on the mark. Your credibility in new home and neighborhood sales is established or lost by your ability to match promises with performance.

So, in the final analysis, it is best to under promise and over deliver. But in the event you can't deliver

UNDER PROMISE AND OVER DELIVER

on a promise, accept complete responsibility and don't make excuses. Instead, be honest, fair, and willing to do whatever it takes to compensate.

"WHEN A CUSTOMER ENTERS MY STORE, FORGET ME. HE OR SHE IS KING OR QUEEN."

JOHN WANNAMAKER

—HE CREATED THE FIRST DEPARTMENT STORE AND PIONEERED THE USE OF PRICE TAGS, MONEY-BACK GUARANTEES, NEWSPAPER ADS, AND WHITE SALES.

PERSEVERANCE

"THERE ARE MANY WAYS TO WIN, BUT ONLY ONE WAY TO LOSE AND THAT IS TO FAIL AND NOT LOOK BEYOND THE FAILURE."

SOCCER PLAYER KYLE ROTE, JR.

PERSEVERANCE 6

The Quick-Fix Mentality

We all have a quick-fix mentality. When facing challenges, we look for instant solutions. We tend to search for the quick book, quick tape, or quick seminar, looking for that one idea that will solve all of our problems.

Suppose you were thirty pounds overweight and I said to you, "I have a technique that will help you lose that weight in one minute or one hour." Would you believe me? The truth is you'd probably be a little skeptical. Yet, we hear claims like this all of the time from those who are selling "snake oil." Don't get suckered in. How long did it take you to get to where you are at this point in your life? Years? Then don't expect overnight changes. It's going to take time to get you to where you want to go. There's no shortcut on the real road to success. You develop by doing and progress by practicing.

People come to me in training seminars and say, "I want to become excellent in selling. What's the one book, one tape, one thing I need to know to become really good?" My reply is always the same: "The one thing you need to know is to give yourself one year."

AVOID THE TEMPTATION OF TRYING TO BECOME THE BEST TOO QUICKLY.

Start a one-year personal growth and development project. Set a goal, develop a plan, and get a series of books and tapes on selling. Above all, avoid the temptation of trying to become the best too quickly. Why? Because, just like a dieter who climbs on the scales daily, expecting to see results too quickly will discourage you. The only thing you should do quickly is start immediately, avoid procrastination, and then give yourself time. There is a season for everything—even success.

As a general rule, reading one book every month will work, while simultaneously committing to a tape series. Then, go out every day and practice what you learn. At the end of the year (not a day, week, or month) evaluate your progress. You will be amazed at how far you have progressed, and shouldn't be surprised if you've tripled your sales.

Be patient and persistent. Don't try to change yourself in an instant. Henry Ford said, "The keys to success are patience and foresight. The man or woman who lacks this is not cut out for business."

Don't Take It Personally

You have probably heard the story of the Wright Brothers. Both were unknown bicycle mechanics who were lacking a formal education. Although they weren't leaders in aviation, they still managed to pioneer the first motorized flight on December 17, 1903.

But do you know the story of Samuel P. Langley? He was a professor of mathematics and astronomy, and a Director of the Smithsonian Institution. Langley was also a scientist and inventor who, in the mid- to late 1890s, actively performed experiments with large unmanned airplane models, gaining notable recognition for his accomplishments.

Because he was at the forefront of aviation, the U.S. War Department gave him $50,000 (an astronomical amount of money for that time) and commissioned him to design and build an airplane that would send mankind skyward.

By 1901, he had successfully tested and created history's first heavier-than-air aircraft. Then, on October 8, 1903, on a modified houseboat in front of journalists and spectators, Langley (with the aid of pilot Charles Manley) attempted to fly his plane, The Great Aerodrome.

ACCEPT LIFE'S CHALLENGES AS LESSONS.

When the launch was attempted, however, the biplane was flung into sixteen feet of water only fifty feet from the boat. Criticism from skeptics and cynics was brutal as evidenced by this report in *The New York Times*:

The ridiculous fiasco, which attended the attempt at aerial navigation in the Langley flying machine, was not unexpected. No doubt the problem has its attractions for those it interests, but to ordinary men, it would seem as if the effort might be employed more profitably.

At first, Langley remained undaunted. Eight weeks later in early December he and his pilot again prepared to make history with their second flight. Yet, once again, disaster struck and this time the pilot nearly died.

As before the cynics and skeptics fiercely attacked the Great Aerodrome, calling it "Langley's Folly," and accused him of wasting government funds. Langley succumbed to his critics and abandoned his project with the heavy-hearted speech, "I have brought to close the portion of work which seemed to be specifically mine—the demonstration of the practicality of mechanical flight. For the next stage, which is the commercial and practical development of the idea, it is probable that the world may look to others."

Instead of throwing his hat in the ring, Langley threw in the towel. He abandoned his pursuit of flight and walked away from his decade-long pursuit. Only a few days later, Orville and Wilber Wright—uneducated, unknown, and unfunded—flew their aircraft from the sand dunes of Kitty Hawk, North Carolina.

Let me offer my perspective of Langley and the Wright Brothers because what happened to them is what occurs in the lives of many people today. Too many allow failure and setbacks to get the best of them, while a few accept life's challenges as lessons and allow their setbacks to propel them toward the achievement of their goals.

In retrospect, it would seem that Samuel Langley had an almost unfair advantage over the Wright Brothers: money, education, reputation, and supporters. Yet, I suggest it was the Wright Brothers who had the unfair advantage over Langley. Samuel Langley had more than his share of cynics and skeptics surrounding his project. As painful as failure can be, it's magnified when others add their ridicule. This would cause him, and anyone else, to emotionalize and personalize their shortcomings. For many, the pain of failure leads to the fear of failure.

Because the Wright Brothers were unknown, they had no cynics or skeptics to criticize their work. The advantage they had over Langley was that, when they experienced setbacks, their thoughts were not on personalized failure but on focusing on the lessons of their failures. Therefore, the first and most important step in overcoming failure (setbacks, obstacles, and challenges) is to understand that failure is an event and not a person. It is something that happens to you that can be demoralizing as well as educational, but it is not you. To put it simply, failing to achieve does not make you a failure.

FAILING TO ACHIEVE DOES NOT MAKE YOU A FAILURE.

If you really want to accomplish your dreams, you must get into the marketplace, take calculated risks, and be willing to experience failure. Soccer player Kyle Rote Jr. noted, "There are many ways to win, but only one way to lose and that is to fail and not look beyond the failure."

Falling Flat on Your Back Makes You Look Up!

I am constantly asked what I think the secret of success is. It's a lot of things, but these two points top my list:

1. Belief in yourself and your mission in life.

2. The ability to persist in the face of defeat.

When you study successful people you will see that they've made plenty of mistakes and have had countless learning experiences frequently disguised as failures. But they have one common trait. Whenever they were at the end of their ropes, they kept hanging on when others would have let go. Much like the Energizer bunny, they keep going, and going, and going.

For inspiration, here are some who didn't know how to quit:

• Dr. Seuss's first children's book was rejected by twenty-three publishers.

• Albert Einstein's Ph.D. dissertation was rejected by The University of Bern because it was "irrelevant and fanciful."

• Noah Webster spent thirty-six years compiling Webster's Dictionary.

• Helen Keller, after losing her sight and hearing as a result of meningitis at age 19 months, became the first blind and deaf person to effectively communicate with the sighted and hearing world. Before age eight, she was an international celebrity. By the time she graduated from college magna cum laude, she was a highly intelligent, articulate, and sensitive woman who labored incessantly for the betterment of others. Overcoming her "double dungeon of darkness," she wrote fourteen books, traveled to thirty-five countries, and met every president from Calvin Coolidge to John Kennedy. Winston Churchill called her "the greatest woman of our age."

• Johnny Unitas, rejected by the Pittsburgh Steelers and cut from the team, kept his dream alive by working construction and playing amateur ball until the Baltimore Colts finally picked him. He eventually became one of the most admired quarterbacks to ever play the game of football.

• Winston Churchill, a person who never quit in a lifetime of challenges and setbacks, may be best remembered for the shortest commencement address ever given. Speaking *"NEVER, NEVER GIVE UP!"* before the graduates of Oxford University he said, "Never give up!" A few seconds passed before he repeated, "Never, never give up!" Then, he returned to his seat.

Turn Your Contacts into Contracts

The undeniable truth is that most new home or homesite sales occur as a result of multiple contacts.

Although many prospects will choose to own during their first visit, the reality is that most sales are completed on return visits to the community, usually after the prospects have already shopped and, by the process of elimination, crossed other competitive offerings off their lists.

It isn't the responsibility of the prospects to come back or call back. They normally won't do it. They will forget you, procrastinate or, even worse, get involved with another salesperson. That's why you must have a strategy to initiate all contacts, callbacks, and appointments. Here are some ways to do that:

- Someone else is interested in your prospect.

- You have a new financing program.

- You're aware of a scheduled price increase.

- They have questions; you have answers.

- You were talking with their real estate agent recently and thought of them.

- You clocked the driving time from the neighborhood to their offices.

- They apologized for not having ample time to spend with you. You want to see if the timing is better now.

- There is an ad running this weekend featuring the home they are considering.

- You just received new information concerning schools, shopping, churches, or neighborhood amenities.

- They have shopped the competition and can give you a competitive analysis.

- They may want to introduce you to their lender or vice versa.

- You have a confidential company report on rising property values.

- You invite them to visit the design center, which may be having a special event with giveaways such as free flags for all veterans, Easter eggs for the kids, photos with Santa, roses for Mother's Day, or key chains for Father's Day.

- There is a new floor plan they might be interested in seeing.

- You share an invitation to play a round of golf.

- Your company is offering special incentives for a limited time.

- A home like the one they wanted just came back on the market.

- You have compiled a housing folder for them that includes all of the home's products and appliances and their warranties. You were just thinking of them.

Your current customers and prospects are also other salespeople's prospects. Therefore, persistence and consistency are the keys to keeping a meaningful relationship. The moment you stop calling or writing is the moment they become involved with another salesperson and builder.

PERSISTENCE AND CONSISTENCY ARE THE KEYS TO KEEPING A MEANINGFUL RELATIONSHIP.

Persistence (with a Strategy) is the Key to Closing Sales

How many "No's" are you willing to take before giving up on a sale?

Before answering, think back to when you were six years old, standing in line with your mother at the grocery store next to the impulse-buying candy counter. The conversation probably went something like this:

"Mom, can I have a candy bar?"

"No, dear."

"Please?"

"No, I said."

You side-step the first two "No's" and begin pleading. "C'mon, Mom. I haven't had one all week...."

Frustrated, your mother responds, "I said no! Now don't ask me again!" Undaunted, you are savvy enough to know that she hasn't really given you a firm reason for refusing to buy you a candy bar, so you persist a little further.

"Why? Why can't I have just one candy bar?" She explains, "Because it's too close to dinner and it will spoil your appetite."

Now you have an objection on which to hang a rebuttal.

"If I promise not to eat my candy bar until after dinner, will you buy me one?" you ask.

What's she going to say? You have eliminated her excuse for not buying you that candy bar.

"Well, I suppose you can have just one. But I want your

promise that you won't touch it until after you've finished eating everything I put on your plate. Do you understand?"

Mom has caved in to your craving.

You probably haven't realized it, but you've been selling since you were a child. And, back then, you didn't quit after only four or five "No's."

When it came to getting that candy bar, you were willing to take the risk to get the

YOU'VE BEEN SELLING SINCE YOU WERE A CHILD.

reward. As you got older, you asked for the car keys, spending money, permission to sleep over at a friend's house, new clothes, Christmas toys, and money for camp. The list goes on. But the bottom line is this: How much money would you be making if your current closing strategy with prospects included the same level of persistence as you gave your poor defenseless mother?

How's Your Resolve?

Each New Year's brings the desire to make (and the potential to break) resolutions. This is the year we'll lose weight, increase our income, stop smoking, eat healthier, make more friends, remove clutter, get organized, have a positive attitude, go to graduate school, take a trip, or exercise.

Our intentions are good, but our resolve weakens the further we get into the year. A 2002 poll reported that 84 percent of Americans make at least one resolution. However, only 28 percent of us follow through in trying to keep them. And, of those who do follow through, 25 percent of the resolutions we do make will be totally abandoned within the first 15 weeks. Those who do manage to make a resolution last for longer than 6 months have usually tried to keep it six times previously without succeeding.

When the parties and cork popping end, we get serious about life. We evaluate where we are and plan courses of action to get us to where we want to be, personally and professionally. Our goals are summarized in the form of New Year's resolutions. They express our ambitions to better ourselves and improve our lifestyle.

While we're very sincere about making them—and well-intentioned—unfortunately, we usually fail to keep them. Why is that? And what's the secret to fulfilling our New Year's promises?

First of all, they are tough to keep because they involve making changes in our lives; and most of us aren't too crazy about change. It scares us because it can be a threat to our sense of comfort. However, if we persevere, as time passes, we begin to see the benefits.

To have a better shot at success this year, anticipate that change has a "down then up" sequence of reactions and understand these four phases of change:

STAGE 1: Denial. This may be characterized by a lack of reaction to the change; it doesn't sink in right away. There can be withdrawal and a tendency to focus on the past.

STAGE 2: Resistance. Strong feelings about the change are evident. They may be in the form of anxiety, frustration, uncertainty, self-doubt, apathy, depression, or anger. Productivity in sales diminishes. There's a tendency to want to quit.

STAGE 3: Exploration. This begins the upswing. You start to draw upon your internal resources and use your creativity to figure out new responses. You become concerned about details and form new ideas, have less confusion, generate more energy, and sharpen your focus.

STAGE 4: Commitment. At this stage, you're ready to act, move forward, complete the mission. You are more cooperative with yourself, better focused, and ready for the next challenge.

> PUT AS MUCH CARE INTO THE END AS INTO THE BEGINNING AND THERE WILL BE NO FAILURE.

Chinese Tao Ta Ching says, "People fail when they are on the verge of success. A tree as big around as a person's embrace begins with a small shoot; a terrace nine stories high begins with a pile of earth; a journey of a thousand miles starts under one's feet; therefore, put as much care into the end as into the beginning and there will be no failure."

Here are some tips for keeping resolutions:

• Put them in writing.

• Set achievable goals. Be specific. Instead of writing a goal saying that you want to sell more this year, write, "This year I will make three more new contacts every week."

• Review your resolutions (goals) every week or month so you can renew yourself.

• Find ways to help you keep your resolutions. If you want to learn more about selling, attend a seminar. Read books. Listen to tapes. Seek out the experts who can support you and move you closer to achievement.

• Make your resolutions attainable. Don't make them so out of reach that you'll get discouraged when you fail to reach them. Change is much easier to manage in little steps.

• Reword previous New Year's resolutions that haven't come to fruition. For example, if a previous resolution has been to lose forty pounds, instead set a goal to exercise fifteen minutes a day.

• Reward yourself with each milestone accomplishment.

• And remember, as Dr. Phil says, "you can't set goals on what you can't control." Make sure the resolutions you're setting are within your area of responsibility and not someone else's. For example. saying, "I'm going to make six people buy new homes this month," Is not an attainable goal because you can't control your clients. The final decision to buy is theirs, not yours. But you can control how you present your new homes, neighborhood and yourself.

Facing Failure

What is the number one cause of failure in sales? Why do most salespeople leave the profession after only a few years? The

OVERCOME THE FEAR OF REJECTION.
answer is that they cannot overcome the fear of rejection. The more value you place on the other person, the stronger your fear of rejection.

Why do we let the fear of rejection negatively influence our behavior? Here are some reasons:

- We're afraid that we may look foolish in front of others.
- We're concerned that others will notice our mistakes and shortcomings.
- We feel that people are evaluating us.
- We worry about the impression we may make on others.
- We are preoccupied about what others will think of us.
- We think we'll do or say the wrong things.
- We're afraid of ridicule.
- We believe that people disapprove of us or what we're selling.
- We expect to hear the word "no" instead of "yes, I'll buy."

How can you tackle this fear of rejection and move on to increase our new home sales? First separate reality from your perception of reality. Not every prospect will be overwhelmed by your sparkling personality. Some may feel indifferent toward you. Others simply may not like you.

If you don't ask for the sale, it is unlikely you will get it. Not everyone you attempt to sell will want to buy from you. The fear of rejection is an attitude issue and can be overcome by strengthening other attitudes—such as confidence, determination, persistence, and your self-image. The fear of rejection is not a technological issue that can be overcome by the latest in electronics. The fear of rejection is a symptom of a need for acceptance, approval, and validation. The fear of rejection sends a loud non-verbal message to prospects that you lack confidence in yourself, your product or service, and your ability to help them solve their problems.

How did we develop a fear of failure? Believe it or not, it may be in our genes. Mentally, rejection translates into social disapproval. Based upon some preliminary research that's been done, we may be genetically predisposed to being sensitive and fearing rejection.

We have always depended upon the goodwill of others for survival. Our country's own welfare system and other government support programs are based upon the Good Samaritan concept of aiding others in their survival. Back in the cowboy-and-Indian days, people traveled in wagon trains so they could form a circle to fend off attacks. Cities were established as people clustered together to survive and benefit from "strength in numbers." Throughout centuries, those who chose to "go it alone" and not depend upon others for survival became outcasts, loners, rebels. By avoiding people, they avoided rejection and the disapproval of others; but they also diminished their chances for survival.

Even today we continue to harbor this inbred genetic fear of abandonment and rejection. We perceive it as a threat to our survival. Although in sales the fear of rejection won't kill us, it does affect our sense of well-being and influences how long we survive and how financially successful we are in the highly-competitive world of sales. Once you realize that the fear of rejection is present within all of us, then what becomes paramount is how you respond to that fear.

Does fear cripple you or catapult you? If you allow yourself to become emotionally wounded by rejection, then you will seek to avoid pain by avoiding the situations that could lead to rejection. Sales calls, meeting-and-greeting prospects, and asking for a sale are all actions that have the potential to end in rejection. Of course, they can also catapult you to success in sales if you perceive that each "no" brings you that much closer to a "yes."

Your behavior in any situation is a consequence of your perception. For example, a couple walks into your new-home showroom. You meet and greet them, introducing yourself and your company.

The husband responds irritably, "Listen, don't bother us. All we want to do is walk around. We don't need a sales pitch. We're just looking around today."

Now, what's your internal dialog? Do you tell yourself, "Fine. They'd be a pain to work with anyway. I'm not going to waste my time"? Or do you think, "They are probably tired from looking at so many model homes. What can I do to make it easier for them? How can I enhance their experience here?"

If you ask for the sale and the prospect responds with, "No. I'm not interested in buying today," do you think, "Great, another rejection. I can't seem to sell anything"? Or do you explain the rejection this way: "He's not interested in buying 'today.' That doesn't mean he won't be interested tomorrow. At least I've established a relationship with him so I can contact him later and get a better idea of what he's looking for."

Failure is Inevitable Sooner or Later

Rejection and failure are entwined. If you try to sell a new home and someone rejects your offer, you think, "I've failed to make the sale."

Therefore, to overcome the fear of rejection, you must first see failure for what it is. Failure is neither negative nor positive. It is simply an event. Some salespeople experience rejection, fail to make the sale, and then quit because they are psychologically crippled. When others fail, they regroup and become better, wiser, and stronger because of failure. What makes the difference is their attitude.

I can sincerely say to you that I've never met anyone who was a major success and had not experienced major failures. To succeed, you must stretch and reach beyond your self-imposed limits, boundaries, and skills. Yet, when you do this, sooner or later you will fail. Speaking from personal experience, I've been there, crashed and burned, but I'm still here writing, consulting, speaking, and selling. It's not that I love to fail, it's just that if I'm not experiencing temporary setbacks occasionally, it's a sign I may be stuck in my comfort zone and not growing.

USE YOUR FAILURES AND REJECTIONS TO CATAPULT YOU FORWARD AND UPWARD.

Learn to use your failures and rejections to catapult you forward and upward rather than complaining about them and quitting. Frank Betcher, one of the great speakers and writers of the last century said, "The price of failure is always higher than the price of success. It always costs more to fail than to succeed. So use your failures as learning opportunities."

Don't Let Rejection Effect Your Affection

Just because someone rejects what you're offering, doesn't mean he is rejecting you. So don't allow it to influence how you feel about yourself. Here are a few suggestions for keeping your self-esteem intact.

JUST BECAUSE SOMEONE REJECTS WHAT YOU'RE OFFERING, DOESN'T MEAN HE IS REJECTING YOU.

• Believe in and have deep affection for who you are—your special talents, personality traits, achievements, etc.

• Surround yourself with people who immerse you in a positive dynamic flow. Avoid the whiners and complainers.

• Make physical maintenance a priority. Take care of yourself. Feed your body right. Exercise.

• Practice stress-reducing techniques.

• Work on maintaining your emotional well-being. Read books that give you a lift and nourish your spirit.

• Focus on your strengths and downplay your weak-

FOCUS ON YOUR STRENGTHS

nesses. Too often it's easy to get into the habit on focusing on our weaknesses in a continual effort to improve ourselves instead of spotlighting those characteristics that make us shine.

• Squash negativity.

• Devise a special way to congratulate and reward yourself for every small achievement.

• Keep a journal of your life and successes. And establish a file in which you can place congratulatory notes, letters from clients, etc. that you can re-read occasionally.

• Be a child every so often and take time to play with abandonment and without guilt.

You Get What You Expect, Not What You Want

When conducting seminars, I share with my audience a true story about a man named Nick.

Nick was a strong, healthy railroad yardman who was consistently reliable on the job. However, he was also a devout pessimist who always seemed to fear the worst.

On one summer day the crews were let off early in recognition of a foreman's birthday. As the workmen left, Nick was accidentally locked in a refrigerator boxcar that was in for repairs. He panicked. He banged with his fists until they were bloody and shouted until his voice went hoarse. Nick reasoned that the temperature in the car had to be near freezing and that, if he didn't get out, he would freeze to death. Shivering uncontrollably, he wrote a final message to his wife on a cardboard box that read: "So cold. Body's getting numb. If I could just go to sleep. These may be my last words."

The next day, the crew opened the boxcar doors and found Nick's body. An autopsy revealed that his body had all the signs of someone who had frozen to death. This was puzzling, however, because the car's refrigeration units were completely inoperable. The temperature inside was around 61 degrees and there was plenty of fresh air. What killed Nick was his perception of reality and his expectations that the worse would happen. And it did.

As tragic as the story is, it does illustrate that many people allow their fears to become self-fulfilling prophecies. In the Bible, Job is quoted as saying, "The thing that I feared most, has come to pass." How true it is with many of us.

An acronym for FEAR is False Evidence Appearing Real. Nick believed the refrigerated boxcar was operating and that he would freeze to death. To him, this became reality. Fear clouded his judgment and immobilized him.

Everyone is afraid at one time or another. Yet, those who have the courage to face their fears will take action in spite of their doubts and uncertainty. You see, courage is not the lack of fear. Courage is the control and mastery of fear.

COURAGE IS THE CONTROL AND MASTERY OF FEAR.

Actor Glenn Ford once said, "If you do not do the thing you fear, then the fear controls your life." You develop courage when you force yourself to take action in the face of fear. So go for that big sale. Try a different approach in marketing. Stop taking "no" for an answer. Stand up and try again. Remember, success is getting up when you fall.

The bottom line? Recognize your fears, but don't resign yourself to them. As Emerson wrote, "Do the thing you fear and the death of fear is certain."

How Dedicated Are You?

Consider the following:

• It took nine years for Henry Miller to write and publish the *Tropic of Cancer*.

• At age 37, Attorney Scott Turow completed *Presumed Innocent*, a novel he wrote while riding on the train commuting to work.

• To reduce his taxes, Henry Miller completed 115 watercolor paintings in five months. He was 71.

• *The Good Earth* by Pearl Buck received this rejection from a publisher: "I regret that the American public is not interested in anything on China."

• An editor wrote this about *The Jungle* by Upton Sinclair: "I advise without hesitation and unreservedly against the publication of this book. It is fit only for the wastebasket."

• H. G. Wells received this response from a publisher when he submitted *The War of the Worlds*: "An endless nightmare. I think the verdict would be 'Oh, don't read that horrid book." Wells found another publisher and this book helped establish him as the father of modern science fiction.

And then there's Doris (Granny D) Haddock. Heard of her? After becoming concerned about political reform, this grandmother—who had emphysema and arthritis—walked across the U.S. in 2000 to support cleaner political campaigns with fewer ties to special interest groups. At age 90, she took her first step on New Year's Day in 1999 in Pasadena, Calif., and walked 10 miles every day for 14 months. She was hospitalized once for dehydration and pneumonia; wore out four sets of shoes; walked during rain and freezing temperatures; and when snows in Maryland and Washington, D.C. threatened to delay her, she cross-country skied one hundred miles along the former C&O Canal tow pathway.

After covering 3,200 miles, she arrived in Washington, D.C., on February 29, 2000, to the cheers of more than two thousand supporters, including several members of Congress who walked the final miles with her. Standing only five feet tall, Doris Haddock cast a huge shadow across Capitol Hill and is credited with demonstrating that Americans really do care about campaign finance reform.

What do Granny D and the others I mentioned have in common? They were dedicated to their purpose. Whenever you want to excel in anything, you must have commitment and dedication. You must say to yourself, "I am willing to pay the price for my success, to commit to the goals I set in life, and to overcome adversities and obstacles that might prevent me from fulfilling my purpose."

Those who succeed do not abandon their goals at the first sign of hardship. They stick to their tasks, remain faithful to their purpose, and become dyed-in-the-wool achievers.

THOSE WHO SUCCEED DO NOT ABANDON THEIR GOALS AT THE FIRST SIGN OF HARDSHIP.

How Can You Become More Dedicated?

• **Be enthusiastic.** Enthusiasm produces a mindset that is empowering and full of self-confidence. It ignites a sense of personal potential and fills you with a spirit of benevolence toward yourself and others.

• **Adopt an "act as if" attitude.** William James, a leading proponent of religious and philosophical pragmatism at the end of the 19th century and who has been called the father of American psychology, said that if you want to cultivate a desired attitude, you must act as though you already have it. If you are a fearful person, act courageous. If you are shy and timid, act confident and out-going.

Jane Marla Robbins, a professional actress who conducts workshops on "Acting Techniques for Everyday Life," has written a book by the same title. In it, she relates the first time she used an acting technique in real life.

> *I found myself in a situation where I had to spend time with a man who it seemed could not be in the same room with me without mocking me, belittling me, or in some way putting me down. His putdowns made me want to shrivel up and die. The times I had to see him became unbearable. Then one day I 'acted as if' he had leprosy. I just told myself, 'I'll pretend he has leprosy," and it worked. For one thing, it helped me to avoid him. After all, I was pretending he had some terrible disease that I could actually catch, so why would I have wanted to get near him? "*

• **Cultivate a burning desire for your primary purpose.** As you grow, you may find your primary purpose changing. That's good. If you're looking for a God-given purpose that transcends all others or you're disoriented about your direction in life, read the bestseller *The Purpose Driven* Life by Rick Warren. The book helps readers answer the question: What on earth am I here for?

• **Identify specific actions** you must take to succeed and establish a plan for completing these actions. Design a daily program of work that is demanding enough to develop your skills and abilities but not so overwhelming that you'll get discouraged and quit.

• **Put yourself on a timeline** so you aren't spread out too thin and become road weary.

• **Don't look for shortcuts.** Success is the result of hard work and dogged determination.

If you've been in new home sales any length of time, you've probably noticed that there are four types of bones working in your office. There are the wish bones, who spend most of their time wishing for what they want; the jaw bones, who are all

WHAT IS YOUR LEVEL OF DEDICATION?

talk and little action; the knuckle bones, who knock everything and everyone; and the back bones, who shoulder the load and get the job done. Which are you? And what is your level of dedication to purpose?

"YOU ARE BEATEN TO EARTH? WELL, WELL, WHAT'S THAT? COME UP WITH A SMILING FACE. IT'S NOTHING AGAINST YOU TO FALL DOWN FLAT; BUT TO LIE THERE, THAT'S A DISGRACE."

ANONYMOUS

Index

A

Ambitious endeavors 5
Lessons for attempting 5
Prepare 6
Trust 7

B

Bad Attitudes 60
Be-backing 53
Beneficial change 91
Blondin (Jean-Francois Gravelet) 5-6
Buffet, Warren 15-17
Burn out 33

C

Change 91
Beneficial 92
Poem about 91
Prevent control 91
Closing
Average 4
Techniques 44-46, 53, 62
Comfort zone 6, 82, 93
Competition 49-51, 73-74
How to approach 50
How to react 50
Reality about 50
Conning instead of selling 113
Consultative selling 45
Coworkers 112
Crab in a bucket syndrome 97
Credibility 125, 127
Customer satisfaction 109, 111, 112, 119, 125
Customer's confidence
Service 109, 112
What they expect from a sales person 118

D

Deadly sin 62
Doomsayer 31

E

Effective coaching 46
Encouragement 82, 85
Empathy 111, 115
How to express 114
Entropy
The doctrine of 33

F

Failure
As a lesson 136, 137, 152
Overcoming 136
Rate 13
Fear
Of rejection 148, 149, 150
Overcoming 8, 24, 150, 152
FEAR
As an acronym 157
Feedback 48, 75, 106, 117
Follow up 44, 51, 54, 110, 119, 120

G

Gates, Bill
Ten Commonsense Rules You'll Never Learn in School 36
Goals 30, 82, 115, 144, 146, 159
Setting 40, 93

About the Author

 Those in the building community are familiar with the name Myers Barnes. He has become America's leading business authority on new home sales and company growth.

A proven leader, popular speaker, and best-selling author, Myers has been called the "most innovative business thinker of our age" and been hailed as "a guru of business reinvention and proprietary systems for success."

As a nationally recognized business insider, he is in touch with the challenges and opportunities confronting companies every day and is able to translate them into a how-this-can-help-you format. His business acumen provides corporate America with a wellspring of knowledge, experience, and tried-and-true strategies.

His company, Myers Barnes Associates, is recognized as a dynamic business resource center for real estate development companies, homebuilding corporations, and sales organizations.

If you want a proven professional who delivers consultancy excellence, has broad experience, and approaches solutions from an integrated perspective, call Myers Barnes.

Myers Barnes Associates, Inc.
Post Office Box 50
Kitty Hawk, North Carolina 27949
Phone: 252-261-7611
www.myersbarnes.com
sellmore@myersbarnes.com